CARING
for
CARERS

JULIA BURTON-JONES

D0610251

Scripture Union
130 City Road, London EC1V 2NJ

© Julia Burton-Jones 1992

First published 1992

ISBN 0 86201 729 7

British Library CIP Data
A catalogue record for this book is available from the British Library.

All Scripture quotations in this publication are from the Holy Bible, New International Version. Copyright © 1973, 1978, 1984 International Bible Society. Published by Hodder and Stoughton.

Book and cover design by Adept Design.

Scripture quotations are from the Holy Bible, New International Version. Copyright © 1973, 1978, 1984, International Bible Society. Published by Hodder and Stoughton.

Printed and bound in Great Britain by Cox and Wyman Ltd, Reading.

For Simon

Contents

1 Home truths   9
2 Tangled feelings   29
3 Where is God in all this?   53
4 If only they understood   75
5 Not enough hours in a day   95
6 A prisoner in my own home   113
7 Thinking big   131
Useful reading   153
Useful organisations   156

Preface

In 1987 I took up a post as Researcher for the Jubilee Centre in Cambridge. Very quickly my research became focused on the needs of older people and their families. I vividly recall devouring texts on caring, feeling a mixture of disbelief and admiration. I began to meet carers in many, varied situations, and to talk to them about their lives.

My research was published by the Jubilee Centre, but I was convinced my task was incomplete, that there was more work to be done in bringing to the awareness of church folk the needs of the carers who were all around them but seemed invisible. For two years I have been training church members up and down the country, helping them to understand the realities of caring at home.

This book is an attempt to help all those people in churches who care about those in need, to get a feel for some of the joys and tensions, pain and commitment, which make up the lives of all those unseen people caring for loved ones at home.

Without the honesty of the carers whose lives are portrayed in it, this book would have remained unwritten. Whilst I have been careful to hide their real identities, I hope I have presented a faithful account of these carers' lives. To meet them has been at one and the same time deeply moving and profoundly challenging.

My thanks are also given to the Jubilee Centre for allowing me to research so thoroughly the issue of 'care in the community' and its effects on families who care. Thanks too to the Scripture Union Training Unit for their support in running the training programme, Action for Family Carers, thereby allowing me to meet the Christians and carers across the country for whose benefit this book is written. Thank you to Campbell Grant, my editor, for his sensitive and constructive advice and gentle wisdom.

Finally, thank you to my husband, Simon, for his ceaseless encouragement and to my parents-in-law and brother- and sister-in-law, whose courage and love throughout their own experiences of caring in the long-term have been an inspiration to me.

Julia Burton-Jones

1. Home truths

I spent an evening with Keith and Janet and then stayed overnight in their home. If ever I inclined towards thinking that caring for a disabled relative has to be an unremittingly negative experience, those hours dispelled the myth.

Multiple sclerosis is one of the crippling conditions that we each dread contracting. We know of its capacity relentlessly and mercilessly to deny its victims the joys and freedoms of able-bodied people. Janet has suffered from it for virtually 30 years. Now almost 50, she was first diagnosed as having MS in her early 20s. Throughout the illness, however, she has never allowed it to dominate her life. One would imagine her conversation to be all of her disability. Nothing could be further from the truth.

Keith is Janet's second husband. They married in 1985, when Janet was 45 and Keith 54, he too being a recent divorcé. Janet's first husband was a policeman. He went to church with Janet, but she says this was only because he was a talented organist and needed an outlet through which to exercise his gift. Janet says he liked to 'have a good time' and was something of a womaniser. It was not easy to have a good time with a wife crippled with MS, comments Janet with irony, and he therefore lacked sympathy with her, she says. He left her for another woman when their son was approaching his teens. He blamed the MS.

Janet's first career was in nursing. Then, in her mid-30s, she retrained as a mechanical engineer. Unfortunately, she was forced by her illness to leave the company for which she worked after just a few years. They still pay her, a decade on, a very good invalidity pension.

Keith's divorce was more recent than Janet's. For many years, says Janet, he endured a marriage in which there was little love. He felt his first wife valued him only for what he could earn. She demanded every last penny from Keith to which she was entitled, following their separation, leaving Keith and Janet very little with which to start their marriage.

Keith and Janet met through a singles club a short time after Keith's divorce came through, eight years after Janet's husband left her. Janet had struggled on with help from devoted church friends in the period since her separation. Somehow she had managed to raise a son, a son who was very fond of her indeed. Keith was working at the time for the GLC and met Janet on a trip to the south coast town in which she lived.

Later, Janet arranged a day shopping in London, and decided, on the off-chance, to ring Keith and suggest they meet for lunch. It was the beginning of a romance which neither could believe to be true. They talked as if they had been great friends for years. A year later they were married.

Janet felt she must tell Keith about the nature and severity of her disability before their wedding. Up to the point when they met, Janet felt very fortunate. She had experienced a couple of bad patches in her illness, during the second of which she had temporarily lost her sight. For the majority of the time, though, she was relatively independent. Her main problem was one of mobility. She had some difficulty walking and could certainly never run. She knew that many MS sufferers were far more disabled after 30 years than she was. So Keith went into the marriage with open eyes. He knew that, while his fiancée's disability was, at that stage, far from obvious, it would worsen in the years ahead. The risks were certainly insufficient to deter him from committing himself to this wonderful woman, whom he loved and admired so much.

The first couple of years of marriage were spent in London. When the GLC was abolished, Keith had to decide whether or not to continue in his position at work. He was feeling increasingly out of place, many of his colleagues being younger, and he so much wanted to spend more time with his new wife. He decided to take early retirement. The next decision he and Janet faced was where to live in their retirement. Both had family connections with a rural part of central England. As both loved the countryside, they decided to move to a small village in the heart of England.

Janet and Keith feel very lucky in having found what is for them a dream home. Their quaint thatched cottage was built in the fourteenth century and still has many of its earliest features. For the couple, who adore history, the last few years, spent in researching the cottage's past, have been both fascinating and enjoyable. Since they began their married life with very little furniture, they have had fun accumulating a houseful of antiques, many of them rare and ancient.

Their shared love of history has manifested itself in a newly acquired mutual hobby. For several years now, Janet and Keith have been avid hunters of antique irons. They now have well over a hundred and are often asked to give lectures on their historical uses. They also both enjoy collecting old china and have some exquisite pieces, many of which were birthday and Christmas gifts to one another, bought with great excitement and tenderness.

A fondness for antiques is by no means all that Janet and Keith have in common. They are each very interested in industrial archaeology, a curiosity born, no doubt, of their working lives; both are engineers by trade. Their fascination with this subject has led them to enjoy together many canal holidays, yet another shared hobby. Indeed, shortly after moving, they bought a small canal barge, but unfortunately were forced to sell it, when the pursuit seemed to be provoking adverse symptoms in Janet.

Finally, Keith and Janet share their Christian faith. While Janet's background has been with the Church of England, she now goes along with Keith to a Congregational church in the local town. You might think that Janet has cause to question a loving God, but she frankly admits that, while from time to time questions do surface in her mind, she has never felt bitter about her MS. Both Keith and Janet derive considerable comfort from their faith in facing some of their struggles. They have been especially blessed by the healing services they have attended which have left them with a sense of peace, if not obvious, or immediate, healing.

As for Janet's condition, it has deteriorated over the course of the last few years. She had a serious relapse two years ago, which had unfortunate origins. Keith has four children by his first marriage, with whom they both get on very well and who have produced for them six grandchildren. On one occasion, when Keith and Janet were staying with one of Keith's daughters, Janet contracted a bad cold. Knowing the ill effects on Janet's MS of infections, the daughter with whom they were staying had ensured her own children were free of colds before inviting Janet and Keith to stay; however, whilst visiting, Keith's other daughter had wanted so desperately her father to see her own new baby that she had come round, regardless of the fact that she and the baby were full of cold.

It was the beginning of a grim couple of years for Janet and Keith. Janet's reaction to the infection was severe. For many weeks she was bed-bound, with scarcely any sensation in her limbs. Consequently, Keith also was tied to the cottage, looking after her as best he could. The recovery has been slow and, as yet, incomplete. The deficit has been, again, in Janet's mobility. She gets around with sticks only with difficulty. If she goes out, she usually takes an electronic buggy with her. Fortunately, the village shop, pub and post office are within a stone's throw of the cottage, so, on a good day, she can buy essentials.

Keith is now working unpaid for a newly conceived business. Because he has no salary, he is able to stay away from work to care for Janet if that is what circumstances require. Fortunately, she usually manages to cope during the day, largely because she has many attentive, caring neighbours, who come round from time to time to check up on her.

Ask Keith if he regrets the months he spent shut up with his ailing wife and his answer will be no. As Janet puts it, they are so fond of each other, that the couple resent the time when they must be apart. Their strongest desire in this world is to spend time together. Their relationship is one of give and take. Janet is still able to help around the house and enjoys cooking especially. Whilst there are many things, some large, some small, for which she relies on Keith, in return she gives him so much that the two perceive no inbalance in their marriage.

If you speak to Janet, she has only loving, warm things to say about Keith. She describes him as a devoted husband. Nothing, she says, is too much trouble for him. He seems more fulfilled now than he has ever been. Talk to Keith, and you do hear protective comments. He is concerned, for instance, not to let Janet do the driving anymore, judging her co-ordination and reactions to be dangerous. In the main, whenever he mentions his wife, however, it is in proud terms. He fondly points out household articles which have some bearing on her past: the sampler she worked as a young child of a thatched cottage; the china bowl in which she was bathed as a baby. He boasts of the three careers she has had: as a mother, a nurse and an engineer.

My impression was of a marriage totally mutual, completely fulfilling. According to Janet, they lack only one thing, a child of their own. Although she was young enough to bear a baby when they were married, Janet has been sterilised. The couple, however, fill the emptiness with the children of friends and with their grandchildren. Besides, they know not to look at the negatives, but to focus on all the good things they share together.

Avoiding empathy

Lost in dreamy prayerfulness, half listening as music prepares you for worship, you sit in a peaceful church, waiting for the service to commence; when suddenly a commotion at the rear of the church disturbs the quietness. You glance behind to see the embarassed expression on the face of a wheelchair-pushing person, struggling down an anything but wheelchair-friendly aisle. But do you read, through the worn lines of that face, the story of a morning spent in devoted preparation of the wheelchair-bound loved one for the trip to church? Do you recognise the effort that was expended in waking, washing, dressing, feeding and transporting that loved one?

For most people, the trials and challenges, the loves and joys, of their own everyday lives, consume the vast bulk of their God-given energies. We need considerable discipline and education before we can begin to enter into another's trials and challenges, loves and joys. Often it is not until we ourselves have been through similar experiences that we can fully understand the situation fellow human beings face. To those who are suffering, each of us can appear unsympathetic and intolerant, not because we are uncaring, but simply because we have not given sufficient thought to what they must be feeling.

Carers often find that the people with whom they rub shoulders are remarkably unimaginative. Professionals, close friends, even relatives fail to comprehend the restrictions and demands of their lifestyle. There are two main reasons for this. The first one is that empathy with carers' problems can be very painful. The second is that, for much of their lives, they are invisible.

Dealing with the first reason, the human condition is very frail. In these health-conscious days, we are only too aware of the many afflictions to which the human frame is prone. We harbour a fear in our hearts of disease and of its consequences. In particular we are afraid for those we love, lest they fall prey to it. From childhood, our dreams are filled with the terrifying possibility that our dearest relatives may be visited by the spectre of debilitating sickness or death. Encounters with those who have been unable to resist the strong hand of illness cause us to shudder and recoil. Our minds have a device that shuts out and blocks morbid thoughts. It does not allow us, for more than a few seconds, to imagine what it would be like if we, or our loved ones, became the victims of sickness.

Is it surprising then that, when we see a person pushing a wheelchair, we do not entertain the thought, 'What if I were in that chair and my husband were the person pushing it?' Were we to meet Keith and Janet in the street, would we readily ask ourselves, 'What if our lives were like that? What if my partner was to develop MS?' Can we expect ourselves to ask, on contemplating the relentless deterioration of someone with dementia, 'What if that were my father and I were caring for him?' This avoidance of thoughts of sadness is a natural defence mechanism, but it is one that we must resist for the sake of those who care for sick and disabled relatives. We must face up to some painful aspects of caring situations, as well as their rewarding, satisfying dimensions, if we are to empathise with carers. To be sensitive to those we know who are caring, we need to become familiar with the details of their lives.

The other reason behind our lack of understanding of carers' needs is the invisibility of their lives. Home is a private place. It holds many secrets. And it is where the majority of caring in families occurs. No amount of curious peering through curtained windows would give us an accurate picture of the life of an infirm person, locked into their home, dependent on the ministrations of their friends and relatives. The front door shuts out our observation and leaves us with only vague notions of what goes on behind it.

The ministering angel

Because carers are invisible, myths concerning their circumstances abound. Carers acquire a kind of 'other-worldly' image. We mistakenly suppose that they number only a tiny minority of our population, that somehow they are different from the rest of us, endowed with angelic qualities which single them out for a life of ministering to the needs of the weak.

In fact caring is by no means a minority occupation. A nationwide government-sponsored survey conducted in 1985 revealed that one in every five households contains someone who has caring responsibilities for a sick, elderly or disabled friend or relative.(1) In more concrete terms, as you look around your church on a Sunday morning, you could expect every fifth pew, or row of chairs, as the case may be, to be filled with people who care for others. As you walk along the streets around the church, in every fifth house you pass, someone will be thinking about the needs of the friend or relative they look after.

When the demands of caring come along, they do not discriminate. They certainly do not select a chosen few who are equal to the task. For many, they are shatteringly unexpected. Expectant parents experience varying levels of optimism as they anticipate the arrival of their unborn child. Some have realistic fears that their baby may suffer handicap because there is a hereditary condition in the family. Others see no cause to worry that something may happen to the child. Whether you are anxiously pessimistic, or without a care in the world, illness or disability could strike. Spina bifida, cerebral palsy and Down's syndrome are no respecter of persons. They strike families of all races, creeds and levels of wealth. Of course, some families choose to include a disabled child through adoption. For them, disability is far from unexpected, it is planned for. This can mean it is easier to cope with, but does not rule out the possibility that adoptive parents could be taken by surprise by the level or nature of caring that is needed.

Sometimes caring situations come about as the result of an accident. A relative may suffer a car crash or an industrial injury which renders them paralysed or brain damaged. Then there are illnesses which may become apparent as a relative reaches adult life. Wasting diseases like multiple sclerosis and rheumatoid arthritis can strike at this stage. So can mental illnesses like schizophrenia and depression, which demand a different kind of caring. As a result of these illnesses and disabilities, we may find ourselves caring for a grown up child or partner.

As our parents grow older, they may develop Alzheimer's disease, or other forms of senile dementia, they may suffer strokes, heart conditions, or merely increasing frailty, and we find ourselves having to make decisions about how we can ensure that they are safe and have all their needs catered for.

Carers are ordinary people to whom the demands of caring have been introduced through the advent of illness or disability in a loved one. They have the same emotions as the rest of the human race. They do not instantly become more patient, more kind, more selfless just because their situation demands it. They know the same frustrations as the average person, they feel the same needs, they have the same reserves of energy. In short, they are not transformed into 'ministering angels' overnight simply because that is what life asks of them.

It is tempting to think that carers do what they do out of choice, and of their own free will. While there is undoubtedly an impulse within most carers to cherish and protect their loved ones in times of illness, they are rarely faced with a choice. Many have the decision that they will become a carer foist upon them, by professionals, by other family members, or simply by the expectations of society around them. We rarely elect to become a carer. Life does not usually give us an option.

The implication of this random distribution of caring responsibilities is that tomorrow you could become a carer. We need to shake off the impression that carers are different, and acknowledge the tremendous upheaval they face in taking on accountability for a sick loved one.

The life and times of a carer

We learned earlier that the world of caring is a very private one, so that how carers spend their lives, once their front doors are closed to our observations, is a mystery to many of us. Most of the up-to-date information we have on caring is to be found in a survey that was carried out for the government in 1985.(2) The data it provides has given researchers, for the first time, an accurate picture of how many carers there are in Great Britain, the characteristics they have and what their responsibilities involve. The survey makes very interesting reading, and is the source of most of the statistics I will use to describe what caring is like. I hope the reader will not find these facts and figures dull. It is necessary to form a picture of caring nationwide, before we move on, in the remainder of this book, to consider the lives of a small number of individual carers.

What carers do

To set the scene for looking at some of the details about what kinds of people care, how many, and for whom, we will take a look at some of the tasks which make up caring. In the survey, practically half, if not more, of the carers interviewed undertook the first four of the following duties.

It may seem an obvious area of help, but one of the tasks listed in the survey was 'keeping the relative company'. In some ways, this part of caring is a continuation of a facet of the relationship that has always been present. In other ways, however, the equilibrium is upset by caring. Disability and sickness can often bring loneliness and isolation in their wake. For the sufferer, spending time away from home can be problematical, if not impossible, so that meeting new people presents an obstacle. As for old friends, and even relatives, visiting can be traumatic and requires discipline, so that sometimes the social network of the person being cared for dwindles. This places a burden on carers to replace the emotional support and stimulation that friends once gave to their relative.

Providing this moral support can be very demanding indeed. Disabled people can understandably be very bitter about the physical pain they experience, and the devastating losses that illness has inflicted (of friends, of employment, of pastimes etc). They look constantly to their caring relative for a shoulder on which to cry, an ear to bend, someone to share in bemoaning the cruel hand of fate on their lives. Mental illnesses like Alzheimer's disease and schizophrenia, and even physical conditions like Parkinson's disease, can bring about personality changes in a loved one. Sadly, some even become hostile, angry and violent towards their relatives, which is hurtful and difficult to tolerate.

17

It would be false, though, to paint an unremittingly bleak picture of the 'being company' dimension of caring. For many carers, it is the very thing that keeps them going. The following is a moving comment made recently by an elderly parent of someone who suffers from cerebral palsy: 'She's been a tower of strength to me. She's the best thing that's ever happened to me. I think that it's her that's kept me going all these years and will keep me going for two or three years more. I can't praise her too much. She ain't heavy, she's my daughter.'(3) For most carers, there is a depth of affection within the relationship which transcends the emotional fatigue of incessant commiseration, the hurts of personal attacks. There is often a tremendous strength to be drawn from the bond between a carer and the one to whom they devote their labours.

Most carers do much more than simply keeping their relative company. They 'keep an eye on them', as the *General Household Survey* puts it. Many sick and disabled people are at risk of harming themselves. Frail elderly people are not sure of their feet and are liable to fall and injure themselves. Confused older people have a tendency to 'wander' (straying into busy roads, for example) or to use household gadgets hazardously (leaving kettles boiling on cookers etc). Similarly, children suffering from conditions like autism have no concept of danger and also need to be supervised. Many carers, therefore, feel that the person they look after cannot be left on their own for more than a few minutes at a time.

A third area of activity for carers is 'taking their relative out'. Many people needing care are wheelchair-bound and need to be accompanied if they are to spend time outside their homes. Others are not responsible enough, due to mental disabilities, to go out alone. If a carer is to guarantee that their loved one does not become cut off from the outside world, they must regularly take them to the shops, to see friends, and to engage in other social activities. This can be a very strenuous exercise requiring both stamina and social nerve!

A fourth set of tasks which the vast bulk of carers perform are essentially practical. You may be able to think of someone who helps an elderly friend or relative with a garden which has become too difficult for them to cultivate. Cleaning, weeding, shopping, cooking, and washing all seem like everyday activities, but they involve extra demands for many carers. For instance, the clothes of disabled people frequently take an unusual degree of wear and tear. You need little imagination to realise that someone with cerebral palsy, for instance, finds it more difficult to get their food from plate to mouth than an able-bodied person would. Inevitably clothes must be cleaned more often than they would be if worn by someone able-bodied. In addition, many disabled people are incontinent, so that their clothes and bed linen need frequent washes. Again, catering can be a bit of a headache. Many people with disabilities have special diets. There are foods which exacerbate their condition and others which are easy for them to digest. Shopping can be complex, cooking separate dishes for different household members complicated and time-consuming.

These four areas of care – keeping a relative company, supervising them, taking them out, and helping them with practical tasks – are undertaken by most carers. The next four sets of jobs are the preserve of the minority of carers who are known as 'co-resident carers'. That is to say, of the six million British carers identified by the *General Household Survey*, roughly one quarter lived with the person they cared for and were, thus, more likely to be giving very much more intensive levels of care than those living in separate households. Several of these activities closely resemble the jobs nurses perform.

Around one half of co-resident carers were responsible for giving their relative medicines that were needed to ease their disability. For some this means simply remembering to give the correct dose of the correct medicine or pill at the correct time. Needless to say, any lapse of memory can have unfortunate consequences. Others, though, have the unenviable task of administering injections – not a job for the squeamish!

Two larger categories of tasks identified by the survey were put under the headings 'personal care' and 'physical care'. Like the last set, many of these duties closely resemble those performed by those in nursing and related professions. This is all the more startling when one considers that most carers are entirely without any kind of training.

In terms of personal care, many carers are required to give assistance to their relative as they get up in the morning. This can involve helping them wash and dress and accompanying them to the lavatory, all of which tasks, the reader will agree, are very intimate and, frequently, embarrassing for both carer and disabled person. Throughout the day the carer may need to help their relative eat meals and go to the toilet. In turn, when bed-time arrives, they will perhaps undress their loved one and help them into bed. Through the night the carer may be called upon to go with their relative to the toilet or change them if they have been incontinent. It is not difficult to understand how these facets of caring can upset the dynamics of a relationship, interfering with the sex life of a married couple, undermining the dignity of an older parent.

A closely related area of responsibility to these personal care tasks, upon which the survey reported, was 'physical help'. This category includes helping a relative with walking. In some cases it means lifting a person in and out of a wheelchair, and turning them over in bed to avoid pressure sores developing. Any nurse will tell you that lifting a sick or disabled person is a very skilled exercise. Because carers are rarely shown the correct way of tackling it, and, in any case, unlike nurses they have no second pair of hands to help, the consequence is that they commonly face injuries – muscle strains in particular.

The final area of responsibility which the survey monitored was in financial matters and areas of paperwork. Some carers have to take on jobs of which a spouse formerly took care, such as paying bills and claiming benefits. It can be frightening and confusing to have to become conversant with technical terms and official documents. Other carers are required to take on responsibility for the financial affairs of a parent with dementia. This means among other things, ensuring that adequate legal arrangements are made for the transfer of assets upon their death, while the parent is still relatively lucid.

Who cares?

It is obvious, having considered the range of roles carers fulfil, from comforter to nurse, to financial manager, to dietician, to gardener, that the demands of caring require incredible versa-tility. I hope this sketch of caring has enhanced the reader's knowledge of the tasks which it involves. Now that we have seen what it means to care, we can ask 'who cares?', 'for whom?' and 'for how long?' Again, many of the answers to these questions can be found in the *General Household Survey*.

Earlier in the chapter, we discovered that no fewer than six million people are caring for a sick, disabled, or elderly relative or friend in Great Britain. In other words, one adult in seven is providing care. A common misconception about caring is that it is 'women's work'. The *General Household Survey* dispelled this myth by showing that 12 per cent of all men in the country were involved in caring, compared with 15 per cent of women. Many of the male carers are, of course, looking after their wives. Most carers are to be found in the 45–64 age group. This is the age at which either one's spouse or one's parents are more likely to be suffering declining health or reduced independence. It seems to make very little difference, according to the survey, which social class you are from, what qualifications you have, whether you are married or not; regardless of these factors, you could find yourself caring for a friend or relative.

As to 'who' carers look after, we noted earlier that one quarter care for someone in their own household. One in every five carers actually looks after more than one person. Four out of five carers are responsible for the care of a relative (the remainder look after neighbours or friends).

If you are looking after someone, you are by far and away most likely to be looking after one, or even both, of your parents or parents-in-law (over half of all carers do). Just over one in ten carers is looking after their husband or wife, whilst three per cent look after a young child, four per cent a grown-up child. Otherwise, you might be looking after another relative, maybe a brother or sister, a grandparent, or an aunt or uncle, or, finally, a friend or neighbour.

The vast bulk of carers (76 per cent) care for someone 65 years of age or older. Similarly, three quarters of the people they care for are female. Again, 73 per cent of caring situations involve a physical disability alone, five per cent a mental disability alone, and 16 per cent both types of disability. The remaining one in twenty handicaps are described merely as the result of old age.

We can see (from these rather arid statistics) that if you are going to be taking on a caring role in the future, it is most likely going to happen to you when you are middle-aged and when your mother, in particular, becomes more frail due to advancing old age. Ironically, this is likely to be the age when your own health starts to decline, so that you are not in the best position to care for another person.

Is caring a short-term experience? Is it a part-time occupation?

The answers to these questions reveal the true nature of the burden under which carers can labour. The survey asked carers how many hours they spend caring each week. In an average full-time job, you would expect to be working 40 hours a week. A very large number of carers 'work' at least 50 hours a week. Most of them do not get Sundays off, either. You may think that, if it were only a short-term commitment, this might be just about manageable. No such luck! You would be fortunate if your caring responsibilities lasted only a couple of years. For some carers, caring can span several decades. Some people really do make a 'career' out of caring, sacrificing their aspirations in other spheres of work, in order to devote all their energies to looking after a loved one.

A carer's work is never done

You might be getting a picture now of the kind of lives carers live. We now move on to look at some of the ways in which caring can so dominate someone's life, that they have opportunity, time and energy for little else.

It is universally acknowledged that life for those in the medical sphere of work can be a hard grind. Nursing shortages mean that many nurses work long hours and have difficulties taking time off. Horror stories of 40, 50, 60 . . . hour shifts worked by hospital doctors shock the news headlines. Hard-pressed though many medical personnel undoubtedly are, however, they at least have times when they can leave their patients and retreat to the unclinical environment of home. For many carers, as we saw in the previous section, home doubles as hospital for sick relatives. And the needs of their 'patients' are unceasing.

Because the demands of caring are ever-present, taking time to relax, to reflect, to recharge and to regain perspective, is almost impossible for many carers. In fact, the *General Household Survey* showed that over half of all co-resident carers had enjoyed no break of at least two days since they started caring. It is scarcely surprising, therefore, that many carers own to feeling perpetually exhausted. Many, too, suffer from stress. In the survey carried out recently by the Spastics Society amongst older parents still caring for a son or daughter with cerebral palsy, over half showed signs of stress.(4) In the same survey, three quarters of carers had physical health problems.

Finding time off for rest and holidays can, therefore, present tremendous hurdles for carers. On the same theme, it can often be hard for carers to sleep well. Many must rise in the night to help their relative use the toilet. Some are caring for elderly sufferers of Alzheimer's disease who are frequently restless at night. Troubled sleeping patterns are something we expect when we have young children, but we do not anticipate that it will be a long-term experience. Some carers have not slept well for years, and this wakefulness, again, has an effect on their emotional and physical resilience.

Most of us take for granted the role of paid employment in our lives. We can even grumble and talk as though we wished it were not necessary. Many carers would dearly love to work, but cannot. Others would like to work longer hours, or progress in their sphere of skill, but cannot. The value of work for carers is that it takes them out of the small, sometimes claustrophobic atmosphere of home, into the wider world, to meet and share the lives of others. Work also gives carers a sense of who they are, of their own identity, in a situation when it is so easy for their own needs and personality to be put on one side in the struggle to sustain another human being.

Another taken-for-granted fibre in the fabric of our lives is our relationships with family and friends. Many carers have to work very hard to find time to maintain friendships with those outside their own homes. They have problems taking time out for social activities, as we remarked earlier. And friends and relatives can be reluctant to visit the home of an invalid. Even other members of the household can feel neglected because of the sheer amount of time that is devoted to looking after the frail one.

Carers, then, can easily lose out on areas of life which others accept as a matter of course. Most of us can choose when and where to take a holiday. Most of us are used to undisturbed, refreshing sleep each night. We usually have the opportunity to work, if we so desire. Most of us, if we make the effort, can sustain strong, mutual relationships with those close to us. We mostly have spare time in which to pursue hobbies. Shopping presents no problem for us. In all of these areas, carers face major obstacles, and later chapters of this book will deal with each in greater depth.

It would be inaccurate to imply that carers receive no help in their task. Many are given sterling support by friends and relatives. Services exist which aim to give them back-up. But, for several reasons, the help available is limited. Often relatives live too far away to offer effective support, willing though they might be. For those relatives living with, or close to, the carer, many are protected from the most rigorous demands of caring by the carer themself, who is reluctant to place upon them burdens which they deem to be their own responsibility. For various reasons, as we shall see in chapter 5, assistance available from other sources is restricted. Resources are limited, so that those in charge of making decisions on behalf of the government will invariably target them towards the growing numbers of frail elderly people in our society living on their own and thus at greater risk than those living with relatives. Also, those services which are available to families with disabled relatives are often designed to meet the disabled person's needs, therefore only indirectly benefiting their carers.

Many carers, as we have seen, are overstretched. Help available to them from the state is limited and relatives and friends are frequently unable or unwilling to make up the deficit.

Caring – an occupation or a relationship?

It may seem to the reader that, in talking about carers as a homogenous group, I put them into an artificial category. Surely, caring is an integral part of all relationships within families? Why should caring for a frail, sick or disabled relative be regarded in a different light? Perhaps, you think, caring should be dealt with simply in books about marriage, parenting and family life.

It is indeed difficult to generalise about caring for a disabled relative. There are as many caring situations as there are carers. Looking after a child with cerebral palsy cannot, in many ways, be equated with caring for a father with Alzheimer's disease. Experiences of caring are governed by a multitude of factors: the relation the carer bears to their disabled relative; the illness or disability of the dependent relative; the stage along the caring journey at which the two have arrived; whether or not carer and cared-for person live in the same house. To talk of carers as if their needs were universal is a pointless exercise.

There are perfectly good reasons, however, for grouping carers together in thinking of ways of offering them support. Increasingly, carers themselves are recognising all the things they share in common with one another. They are becoming a growing movement, determined to achieve public recognition. The Carers National Association, the national charity for carers, has succeeded in recent years in giving carers an awareness of their identity.(5) Many of their local branches are becoming militant in demanding adequate services and financial recompense. Through these branches, carers are also giving one another much support and advice.

Carers within this new movement are speaking with one voice about their many needs, expressing similar concerns, regardless of their circumstances. If carers themselves feel there is value in belonging to each other in a group, there must surely be value in discussing their corporate needs in the context of the support individual Christians can offer them.

The focus of the book

The premise upon which this book is written is that Christians can, and should, offer help and encouragement to those who struggle with their lives as carers. In Galations 6, verse 2, we find the injunction, 'Carry each other's burdens and in this way you will fulfil the law of Christ.' Paul also says in Roman 12, verses 10 and 15, 'Be devoted to one another in brotherly love. . . . Rejoice with those who rejoice; mourn with those who mourn.' Jesus, in Matthew 11, verses 28–29, calls upon those who are weary and burdened to come to him. In these and many other passages in the Bible, we are called upon to care for those in need. I believe that in caring for the carers in our congregations and communities we are fulfilling God's law and demonstrating powerfully the love he feels for each of them, thus pointing them towards our heavenly Father.

It is easy for us as Christians to take for granted the desire of families to care for their sick and disabled members. Through this assumption we fail to see that many families lack the resources to care single-handed. Some individuals who feel compelled to care are so frail that they themselves need care. For those who genuinely want to carry on caring, but cannot continue alone, churches can help. For those who have reached the end of their capacity to provide physical care, we as Christians can offer support during the heartbreak of letting go.

Much of the information given in *Caring for Carers* is based upon the true stories of carers I have interviewed through my research. Caring, in the book, is therefore seen uniquely through their eyes. The following chapters are not an objective critique of specific situations, but a description of the way in which a handful of carers perceive their own lives; for this, I make no apology. In some cases my interviews were with both carer and their dependent relative. But, in most, I spoke only to the carer. My accounts of their circumstances may sometimes, therefore, reflect only indirectly the concerns of their disabled relatives.

I have attempted to include carers with widely varying experiences. Some care for disabled children, others for spouses, others for parents. The conditions of their relatives are sometimes mental, sometimes physical. Not all the carers I include are Christians, most are. They come from all over England, some from affluent areas, others from poorer parts, some from rural communities, others from cities. It is impossible, in describing the lives of a handful of people, to present a representative picture of caring. The goal has been simply to help you to put yourself in the position of the carers you know, and to help you imagine some of the struggles they face, so that you can then know how to offer help.

I have found the process of meeting and talking with carers all over the country, through the course of writing this book, immensely moving and challenging. I hope you will feel the same admiration I feel for each one of them as you are introduced to them. Chapters 2, 3 and 4 are all about the unseen problems carers face. We will look at the feelings caring can provoke in chapter 2. In chapter 3 we will consider some of the spiritual dilemmas which caring can bring about, while chapter 4 looks in detail at the effects caring can have on a person's relationships. In chapters 5 and 6 we focus on the practical problems carers face and the difficulty they have in taking time off. Finally, in chapter 7, we will give examples of some of the many things churches can do and are doing in offering support to carers.

I hope that, through reading what follows, you will realise that there are many ways in which the help you can offer could make all the difference in the lives of the carers around you who struggle with the responsibilities they carry.

References

1. OPCS, *General Household Survey 1985*, HMSO, 1988.
2. *ibid.*
3. Virginia Alison and Fay Wright, *Still Caring*, Spastics Society, 1990, p 2.
4. *ibid.*
5. Carers National Association, Head Office, 29 Chilworth Mews, London W2 3RG.

2. Tangled feelings

Tom and Dot were childhood sweethearts. They first met each other in their early teens and became boyfriend and girlfriend a couple of years later. They married in 1950 when Tom was 23 and Dot 22. Tom is proud to say that Dot was the only girlfriend he ever had.

Would Tom, if he had known what was to happen to his beautiful young bride, have had second thoughts about marrying her? An idle question it may be, but in making (perhaps too glibly?) our vow to care for our partner in 'sickness and in health', we rarely make a conscious commitment to stand by our beloved through the possibility of an agonising illness like Alzheimer's disease.

In the first 34 years of their marriage, Dot and Tom were never, in fact, brought face to face with the implications of that wedding vow. They enjoyed the best of health. Tom swears that Dot never complained of suffering so much as a headache and had certainly taken no days off work for illness. Being a great sportsman, he, too, had been extremely fit.

Then, out of the blue, in 1984, Dot began to do strange things. The change that came about is marked in Tom's memory by an occasion when his wife attempted to boil eggs in a dry pan. Then he noticed that her concept of time was affected. She would prepare Tom's tea at odd hours. She was only 57 and Tom could not face the possibility that Dot's mind might be sick. He tried to ignore her strange behaviour and memory lapses but knew in his heart of hearts that something was badly wrong. This period of growing awareness of his wife's illness remains in Tom's mind as the worst time of all. He knew only too well that an older brother and sister of Dot's had suffered from Alzheimer's disease, but was horrified by the suggestion that his cherished wife might be going the same way.

Tom felt very alone in his suffering. To the outside world, there did not seem to be too much wrong with Dot. She looked a picture of health and even managed to continue working part-time. She retired in 1984 from the electronics company where she had been a valued member of staff, but continued for several years working as a cleaner for the city university under the supervision of her sisters-in-law.

Sadly, Tom felt his GP failed him. Had the doctor acted more responsibly, Tom sees now, his experience of caring could have been so different. Dot herself refused to accept anything was wrong with her and the GP said there was nothing he could do without Dot's consent. It seemed as though no one, neither relatives, nor professionals, understood the heartache Tom was experiencing. Isolated and driven to distraction coping with a sick wife, Tom reached rock bottom. He even considered committing suicide and taking Dot with him. Around about this time, Dot sprained an ankle out cleaning. Tom was overjoyed when she agreed to visit the doctor for help, anticipating that at last her more fundamental problem would be identified and help would swiftly follow. 'You look well for your age! I hope I look as well as you do,' was the doctor's remark. Although it was not their own GP, Tom had hoped some mention of the concerns he had expressed earlier about Dot's health would appear in her notes. No reference to them was made, however, and once more Tom was left feeling that no one in the world grasped the reality of the situation he faced.

It was not until 1989, five years into Tom's ordeal, that he was eventually put in touch with an effective support system. A neighbour, whose husband was a stroke victim, mentioned Tom's plight to her social worker. The social worker visited Tom and, realising the enormity of his problem, contacted his GP, who was, by this time, a young woman, his former GP having died. Help came swiftly from that point onwards. In September 1989, shortly after finishing her cleaning job, Dot was diagnosed as having Alzheimer's disease.

An unfortunate incident which had occurred in the summer of 1989 was to have a profoundly damaging effect on Dot, worsening her mental condition markedly. Out on an errand to the local shop, she had been knocked down by a lorry. Failing to see Dot, the driver had backed into her on the pavement, sending her hurtling into a wall some 10 feet away from where she had been standing. Although released almost immediately from hospital, she had sustained an injury which could have proved fatal.

In November, in a routine brain scan to assess the extent of the dementia, doctors were amazed to discover two blood clots on Dot's brain. Tom had noticed changes in his wife – her eyes had become very dull, among other things – but had attributed them to the Alzheimer's disease. Now it was obvious that immediate action was necessary. Tom had to consent to an emergency operation conducted only hours after the neurologist's first meeting with the couple.

The operation was a success, but sadly Dot's condition has worsened dramatically since the accident. Tom has made it his business to acquire knowledge about Alzheimer's disease. He belongs to the Alzheimer's Disease Society, has read books and attended conferences on the illness, and talked to professionals in the field. The result is that he now knows what to expect in the future and can see how Dot has passed through many of the phases Alzheimer's patients endure. Initially it was Dot's memory that was lost. She would also suspect people of stealing things from her. She was like a squirrel, Tom says, too. She would wrap things up and hide them away in obscure places so that, in some cases, Tom would not find them again for several years. She would turn on the gas oven without igniting it.

In 1987, Tom began to see signs of the next stage in the illness, what he calls the 'wanderlust'. Dot began to disappear and would be found wandering miles from her home. This phase reached a climax in 1989 and was the most trying of all the problems. If Tom was not constantly vigilant, Dot would be out of the house in an instant. Throughout this phase, two further symptoms began to emerge. The first was one of continence. Dot became doubly incontinent, a factor which altered the form of care she needed from Tom dramatically. Also, she gradually lost the ability to speak so that she is now able to say nothing.

Up until this time, Tom was able to continue working full-time. He worked as a clerk of works for a housing association in the neighbouring city. Tom started out in the building trade, as a bricklayer, at the age of 14. He spent 10 years attending night school, learning skills which were to serve him well throughout a 50 year career in the construction industry. Tom loves his work. He has strong views about it, believing the need for good housing to be the most important human need of all.

Tom struggled on as long as he could, returning at 5.30 pm each day to face a gruelling evening of changing and cleaning Dot, preparing supper and somehow fitting in the time for washing, ironing and housework. Eventually it became too much for him and he began in 1990 to work part-time (from 8.30 until lunch-time each day). Dot spends the mornings during the week in a local authority home where she has her breakfast and lunch.

Tom now feels fortunate to have access to a range of support services. It was through Dot's hospital assessment in 1989 that Tom became aware of the help he could receive. He speaks highly of the consultant psycho-geriatrician at the local hospital who has given Tom two weeks' respite care for Dot when he has become over-tired. The consultant has also helped Tom fight for Mobility Allowance, a benefit denied him several times, but granted eventually by a tribunal in January 1991. Through the hospital Tom has received the advice of a community psychiatric nurse who has helped Tom receive continence pads that are far more effective than the ones previously supplied by the district nurses.

He still has moments of frustration caused by the inertia or incompetence of professional people. An occupational therapist agreed, when she assessed Tom and Dot's home, that they needed special rails and a shower in the bathroom. Tom had too many savings to qualify for a shower, but the rails were promised. While they waited to have hand rails fitted, however, Dot had a nasty fall in the bath and broke her nose. It was a traumatic experience for Tom, dressing her as she bled profusely, and rushing her to the hospital. In his exasperation, Tom went out the very same day and bought, out of his own resources, the items required to make the bathroom secure and, that evening, fitted them himself.

It was after Dot's diagnosis that Tom's relatives came to the dawning realisation that he was struggling at home. His brother lives in the next street and now calls in to see Tom every evening for half an hour and shops with him for a couple of hours on Saturdays. His wife cooks Tom's main, lunch-time meal of the day and takes it round when Tom gets in from work and at the weekends. This is a great help, as it means Tom only has to cook a snack in the evenings.

Tom can see that Dot has now moved into the next stage of

Alzheimer's disease. Far from wandering constantly, she is now unable to stand on her own. He has to lift her from her chair and push her up the stairs to the bathroom when she needs changing. Once in the bath, he has to exert considerable strength in pulling her out. The incontinence is now a part of life. The day before I visited was the worst of all. Dot needed changing three times. Tom admitted to feeling so exasperated with Dot that he almost hit her. Of course, he felt very remorseful, but in that heated moment there was a real risk of him lashing out at Dot.

Because Dot is now unstable on her feet, she falls frequently, injuring herself quite badly. She strangely feels no pain, though, so does not complain, even on occasions, such as one several months ago, when she fell backwards and fractured her skull. The constant trips to casualty are very stressful for Tom, who is in a state of exhaustion anyway. He gets up at around 2.30 am every night to take Dot to the toilet or to change her. He then get up at 6.15 am, cleans and dresses her, taking her to the toilet. At 8.00 am he leaves Dot at the old people's home and sets off for work. At 1.00 pm he collects Dot. He puts her on the commode (which is downstairs), and, if necessary, changes her. At 6.30 pm he then changes her pad and clothes again. Dot's incontinence generates mountains of washing and ironing. As Tom said, she needs treble the amount of clothes others have, as she wears three outfits a day. This costs Tom a lot of money as well as effort. Dot can no longer feed herself, so that Tom has to feed her.

By far the hardest thing about caring for a wife with Alzheimer's disease, says Tom, is the loneliness. He says he would much rather Dot's illness were a physical one. At least then he could still talk to her. At the weekends, he can spend hours exchanging no words with anyone. He is so grateful for his brother's regular visits. Another friend who comes round faithfully for a chat on Saturdays is someone with whom Tom started a judo club back in 1950. Other friends, though, do not come anymore. The couple have no children and Dot's own living relatives have never shown any concern, let alone visited.

There are opportunities for Tom to spend time away from home, when Dot is in respite care, but he does not have the heart to go away on holiday and leave her, or even to have a night out at the pub. Tom is grateful for all the help he receives, only wishing he had known early on what he knows now. However helpful the people who visit are, though, he recognises that he is the one left with Dot, providing the care, when they leave.

Despite the many trials and the absence of rewards, Tom dreads the time when his wife's condition is so severe he can no longer look after her at home. He can hardly bear to think of Dot as she was, but says she was a devoted wife. Tom used to spend most of his evenings and weekends involved in the sport he loved so dearly, and she never once complained. Although they did argue occasionally, in 41 years of marriage they never had what Tom calls a 'sulky row'. He glows with pride as he remembers how spotless she kept the house, while working full-time, how she did all the cooking and baked her own bread. She was a very attractive woman, he boasts, and wore only the best clothes. He claims he has never heard one criticism of his wife, who was a lady always ready to help those in need, to the extent that he wonders if there can be a god in heaven who would allow her to come to this. He spent some time looking at old photos of her recently, but the memory was so painful he had to put them away again.

Tom's care of Dot is devoted. He respects her dignity totally, making sure she is always clean and continuing to buy for her the expensive clothes in which she always took pride. He knows only too well how horrified Dot would have been if she could have seen the state she is in now. He cannot visit her in hospital — his urge is always to take her home and care for her in the way he alone can. He recognises his efforts are futile, in one sense, in that one day soon Dot will die, but the only defence he has is to avoid facing up to that reality. At moments when he is likely to start thinking too deeply about the tragedy of the situation, Tom finds something to do to take his mind off it. His small consolation is in knowing that Dot still just about recognises and feels at home with him. He is determined to keep her in the home they have shared now for almost 40 years for as long as possible. But he admits that life will be tough next year when he retires and spends all his time at home. A solace is reading. He enjoys books on the theory and practice of building and whiles away many an hour spent sitting on the stairs waiting for Dot to use the toilet with his head buried in a book. He will continue reading books on building when he retires.

The future does not look rosy. Tom knows Dot will soon reach the stage when she spends most of her time sleeping. Then will come the phase when she stops eating. For now, he lives a day at a time, striving to give the ultimate care to a woman to whom he feels he owes a debt of gratitude and who will never be able to repay him. The dreams he had cherished, towards which he had saved for a lifetime, of a retirement spent in healthsome activity with a beloved wife, have evaporated. Gone are the times when they holidayed happily together in hotels in Bournemouth, or in later years, caravanned in Skegness. No more are the pleasant Saturday evenings when the couple would go out for their customary meal in a local hotel or restaurant. 'All the money in the world's no use to us now,' says Tom sadly.

The feelings caring provokes

Emotions lie deep at the heart of any caring relationship. Such a relationship may well have its outworkings in practical activity, but at its root, as its impetus, is an emotional bond.

Those who have attended meetings for groups of carers cannot doubt that caring is an occupation highly charged with emotion. Wave upon wave of intense feeling will ripple across the group. Warmth of love, and heated anger, merge. Tears are shed openly, pain is inconcealable.

Common themes emerge from accounts of the emotional dimension behind caring. At this point, however, we must note the variety in responses, before moving on to a consideration of the key common elements. We each react differently to the events of which the fabric of our lives is composed. Some of us revel in change and enjoy new challenges. Others of us prefer the security and predictability of routine, finding upheaval traumatic. Our reactions are fashioned both by temperamental factors and by past experiences. Some will consequently greet the onset of caring responsibilities with optimism and cheerfulness, while others will experience alarm and fearfulness. We must expect every carer to make a unique response to the demands of their role. Neither should we assume that every carer is in need of help. Many are coping well. Only by knowing and understanding the carer will we have insight into their feelings.

Another key to understanding the feelings provoked by caring in each individual is to refer to the relationship they bear to the one for whom they care. The feelings associated with marriage are, of course, of an entirely different nature from those linked to the parent–child relationship. Caring in these two different contexts will, of course, have differing emotional connotations. In the same way, caring between brother and sister, grandparent and grandchild, friend and friend, is a unique experience. We must not anticipate that responses across these varying relationships will be identical.

Yet another factor influencing the feelings of any carer will be the stage along their caring journey at which they have arrived. We might expect that some of the circumstances causing pain are particularly acute in the early stages of caring. On the other hand, the stage at which caring needs perhaps to be handed over to another person or a more suitable environment could provoke a new set of feelings, some causing hurt. The important truth to remember is that feelings are not static; they vary from year to year, month to month, day to day, even minute to minute. We are less able to help if we are attempting to address a problem which is no longer an issue. It is, thus, impossible to make generalisations about the feelings experienced by carers. They will vary according to their personalities, the quality or nature of their relationship with their disabled relative, and the stage in the caring process at which they have arrived, among other things. We can expect a varied response, therefore. But we can also expect a complex response.

The emotional effects of caring are typically complicated. Many carers harbour in their souls a storm of conflicting feelings. It is possible to experience simultaneously towards another person deep love and dark anger. These tensions in the lives of many carers drive them to distraction. We should avoid reaching hasty conclusions about the sentiments of a carer. It is important to recollect that, whilst they might be expressing resentment towards a dependent relative, beneath the surface of their anger is resilient affection. If we can help the carer resolve, or at least learn to live with, the inner conflicts, we have achieved a lasting good.

The rewards

Were we to examine first the less pleasurable feelings connected with caring, we might find ourselves faced with the question, 'what makes them carry on?' It is hoped that, by prefacing discussion of the negatives with a description of some of the benefits caring offers, we will be able to understand where the ability to endure hardship springs from.

In some respects, caring informally for a relative or friend mirrors the role played by nurses, doctors, social workers and others who are paid to look after others in society. In crucial ways, however, there are differences. Opting for a career in, say, medicine allows greater choice than being faced with a situation where to care for a relative full-time seems to be the only available choice. On the other hand, the motivation to care for a loved one who is sick surpasses even the strong impetus that many professional people possess to protect and minister to those in need. In short, caring at home for many people fulfils a strong urge in carers to respond to the needs of those close to them.

In human terms, you might say that to care is a human instinct. It is natural for us to provide for those near to us by blood or marriage. Within us, for example, is the drive to nurture our young. In the same way, we have an urge to defend our weaker relatives. In divine terms, the ability and desire to care for others is God-given. We find fulfilment, as a human being made in the image of God, only in serving those around us. To care for them is to obey God, and to obey God is to find life in all its fulness.

For many people, caring for others gives meaning to life, therefore. It gives a sense of identity, of having a valuable contribution to make in society. It is important in this context to remember that the disabled person, no less than their carer, has the instinct to care for others. For them this need is harder to meet, but one which is nonetheless crucial in giving a sense of self-worth. We need to find ways of helping carers which do not put their disabled relatives forever on the receiving end of kindness. We need to discover life-giving ways of allowing disabled people to know and to feel that they are giving to the society around them. Only then will their humanity in God's likeness be appropriately affirmed.

So the instinct to care is integral to being human. Caring for a close relative can be fulfilling and enjoyable for this reason. But not only is caring a part of being human, it is also part of a relationship. Herein, most often, is found the reward of caring. Keith and Janet's relationship, described in the introductory chapter, illustrates this point extremely well.

For Keith, caring for Janet is positively pleasurable. The occasions when her multiple sclerosis is especially bad give him an excuse to spend time with her. The love they share is so enriching that looking after one another seems effortless. For the many other carers of spouses, their marriages are often of such companionship, harmony and compatibility, that seeing their partner through periods of ill-health and disability is something which they do gladly. While outsiders observe only an inbalance in the relationship, carers will speak thankfully and affectionately of the emotional support they receive from their partner. The caring is an opportunity perhaps to fulfil a vow made many years ago at their wedding ceremony to look after their husband or wife in 'sickness and in health'. In such marriages there is a sense of romance and mutual respect which survives, even deepens, through the pain of ill health.

For carers of disabled children, their caring is an extension of the commitment we each make to our offspring. It is part of the protectiveness we feel towards our babies and young children. I speak to so many parents of disabled children who delight in their sons and daughters. So many say that life would be dull, humorless, meaningless, without their child.

A different joy is awakened through looking after an elderly parent. It is the happiness of finding at last an outlet for the gratitude for a life-time's practical and emotional support. For these carers, to provide high quality care is to say thank you to a mother or father for sacrifices made.

Would that these positive experiences of caring were universal and unmixed with painful emotions. Unfortunately, few carers encounter caring in the way Keith, in the first chapter, has. It is common for carers to feel one or more of the unpleasant sensations described below.

The grief

For Tom, and for many carers, the predominant feeling is grief. Coming face to face with a situation which initiates caring is nothing short of a bereavement type of experience for many.

There can be an overwhelming sense of loss. The carer witnesses someone they love become another person. Hopes for the future are torn apart. For Tom this was a slow, destructive process. Before his eyes, he witnessed the attractive, capable wife of his youth and middle years become a disorientated, dependent old lady. Initially, random actions and attitudes were out of character. Now Dot is no longer the vivacious, caring person she was before Alzheimer's disease struck. Tom can scarcely bear to look at photographs of Dot as she was – feelings of loss overwhelm him.

The experience of loss is particularly severe for carers of mental illness sufferers like Dot, but is also common amongst those whose relatives fall victim to physically disabling conditions. Those with disabled children can only dream about the aspirations they cherished for their son or daughter. For carers whose partners fall ill, there is a mourning for the husband or wife who was able to contribute more to the relationship, in sexual, practical and emotional terms. Again, to see a parent's decline provokes grief for the mother or father of our childhood to whom we looked for support and protection. For carers going through feelings of loss, memories can be acutely painful. We can only imagine the agony Tom feels when he looks back on the plans he and Dot fondly made for their retirement years.

In the initial throes of caring, the feeling of loss extends to other areas where the carer feels they have been required to make sacrifices. Perhaps they have given up paid employment to devote time to caring, in which case they will miss the stimulus of work and friendship with colleagues. Maybe other relationships or pastimes can no longer be sustained, and the carer yearns for them.

The initial sense of loss in the early days of caring can easily give way to a despairing sadness. To be continually confronted with the struggles and suffering of a dear loved one can demoralise. The future can look unbearably bleak from the viewpoint of someone caring for a chronically and incurably sick person. Things, it seems, can only get worse.

The sadness is mitigated by circumstances. Tom's situation is excruciatingly demanding in a physical sense, and, for much of the time, he is exhausted. The tiredness is exacerbated by Dot's incontinence which disturbs his sleep during the night. Stress, exhaustion and lack of sleep lower our emotional resources. They lower our resistance and cause us to lose perspective. Small problems seem disproportionately large and unmanageable. In extreme cases, such as Tom's, they can contribute to the carer feeling suicidally depressed. In his state of lowered resistance, Tom could offer no defence to his sense of the futility of life. It seemed that to kill himself, and his wife, was the only solution.

Tiredness is not the only factor contributing to despair. Many painful feelings become intolerable because there is no one upon whom the carer can off-load their sadness. The person on whom the carer previously depended may well be the one whose illness is now causing them distress, and is thus not in a position to offer the help needed. Neither does any one else seem to recognise the sadness the carer feels. Sadness turns to despair.

The anger

A feeling closely linked to depression is anger, something many carers admit to feeling. Their anger has many sources, depending on the individual concerned.

In the early days, the anger may be directed at no one in particular. It is a response to the apparent injustice of the situation itself. It seems unfair that my daughter should have to endure such pain and dependency, when other children are strong and carefree. It does not seem right, thought Tom (like many others), that my wife, such a good and caring woman, should be rewarded for a lifetime's kindness with this crippling illness.

As caring progresses, new causes for anger emerge. In Tom's case, anger was directed at the GPs who failed to recognise or do anything about Dot's illness. Tom, and many other carers, feel annoyed that supportive services are scarce and inadequate. For many months, Tom struggled with continence pads which were too small, simply because they were less expensive than the larger, more absorbent pads Dot now has. Rails to help Dot shower were not supplied in time to spare her what could have been a very serious accident. Tom, enraged, installed the rails himself.

The sad truth of the matter, however, is that the largest part of the anger carers experience is directed very often at the loved one for whom they care. Sheer exhaustion and frustration alone drive people like Tom, and Sarah, who we will meet later in the chapter, to shout at and even physically assault their disabled relative. It may be the behaviour of the disabled person which is maddening. Alzheimer's patients can go through very restless phases, when they cannot sit still. Often they repeat the same meaningless phrase or question over and over again. In cases like Tom's, it is the frequent incontinence which can drive a carer mad. How easy it is, when driven to distraction, to react violently to such behaviour. For some carers, it is not so much the behaviour as the attitude of their relative which can provoke anger and resentment. We shall see how Sarah's mother's negative responses incensed her carer. When illness or pain cause a person to become demanding, bad-tempered or moody, their carers often respond irritably. There is a real risk that a frail person will be injured, then, at the hands of an angry carer.(1)

It is an irony that those we love the most are the people who tend to provoke in us the most intense anger. The dynamics within caring are subject to the same principle. They will be influenced by the nature of the relationship between carer and disabled person historically. Relatives who have always irritated us are likely to continue to irritate us, even when we care for them, perhaps then especially so!

Carers often feel bitterness and resentment towards their other relatives and friends too. They may feel that a brother or sister is not playing their part in caring for their disabled parent. They may feel their husband or wife has the wrong approach to caring for their child who is disabled. Whatever the cause, disharmony causes bitterness for many carers.

The guilt

Many carers despise themselves for feeling anger and resentment towards someone who is enduring great suffering. They feel their soul must be capable of great wickedness, that they are unworthy. Their self-esteem drops to a very low level.

Many set themselves impossibly high standards. When they fail to reach these standards, and they think that the caring they are giving is substandard, they feel a second level of guilt. They do not recognise that too much is asked of them, that too little support is available to them. They see only that they could be doing more, and reproach themselves.

The anxiety

The guilt frequently forms for carers an element of a broader sense of anxiety. Sarah's anxiety that she is not offering the appropriate kind of care for her mum, as we will see later, is part of an overall state of worry she feels concerning her mum.

The anxiety carers feel manifests itself on a micro level, but is also felt on a macro scale. On the micro level, carers constantly worry when they are apart from their disabled relative. They fear that accidents may have befallen them. Tom must have worried, while out at work, that Dot would leave on the gas, or wander onto a dangerous road. Sarah must be anxious that her mum will carry out her threats of suicide.

The nature of this micro level anxiety will depend, in large part, on the nature of the dependent relative's illness or disability. For carers of mental illness sufferers, there is a constant fear that the person will do damage to themself. For some, there is also a fear that the relative will harm another person, even oneself. For carers of physically disabled people, the fear is that they will perhaps fall and be hurt. Many carers are preoccupied with worry that circumstances beyond their control will adversely upset arrangements. Will they collect Mum for the day centre on time? Will my employers continue to accommodate my special needs as a carer? Will the authorities make the right decision about my child's education? . . .

Much of the worry carers feel, however, is at the macro level. This worry is, perhaps, even more difficult to handle. It is anxiety which relates to the future, often the long-term future. Rightly or wrongly, it is common for carers to feel they are indispensable. Their disabled relative may indicate that only their caring relative will do, when it comes to being looked after. The carer feels that they alone understand how their relative likes things: the cup of tea first thing in the morning; the TV quiz show in the afternoon; the daily walk in the local park.

Inevitably, then, hanging over the carer is the fear of what would happen to my child, my wife, my father, if ill-health or death were to separate us. Many carers dread health problems for fear of what would happen to their disabled relative. This anxiety is perhaps most pronounced for carers of disabled children. They know that, in all likelihood, they will die before their son or daughter. Many can scarcely face the thought that their child might then be placed in a residential home. For an elderly spouse, the fear is similar, with many older carers expressing the hope that their husband or wife should go first.

As a consequence of this anxiety, and of the intensity of demands and lack of proper rest they experience, many carers show signs of extreme stress.(2) These, frequently physical symptoms of anxiety, are unpleasant, damaging to health, and can often become ingrained. If they are left untreated they can result in 'breakdown'. I recently met a carer who had long since ceased caring full-time for her sick mother. Her nerves, however, had become so fraught, through the experience of caring, that she was in need of long-term counselling from a local Methodist minister. Sadly, many carers' mental health collapses when caring ceases. It is as if their concern for their loved one has pushed them beyond the boundaries of human tolerance.

Sarah has recently bought a brand new studio flat in a Middlesex suburb of London. It is only tiny – little more than a 'glorified bed-sit', as she sees it – but, at 40, she at last has a place to call her own, after many years of renting shared houses.

An only child, Sarah left home at 18 to study at university and never returned. She has lived, throughout her working life, as a librarian in London, and has no inclination to leave the city. She is a resourceful, independent person, who seems happy with her own company.

Amanda, Sarah's mum, is a different person altogether. She left her parents to marry in her early 20s and has never worked. Her life has, therefore, been very much home-based, and she has derived her sense of identity from the people for whom she has spent her life caring, namely, husband Ted and daughter Sarah. She is a 'worrier' by nature, says Sarah, and this tendency for anxiety to become out of proportion led her to suffer a serious depressive illness some time ago. Indeed, the pressure of his own job as a teacher, added to the stress of caring for a depressed wife, contributed to Ted's own breakdown shortly afterwards. Ted found he was not equal to the task of returning to teaching after his recovery, and instead took early retirement.

Amanda was glad to have Ted around the house more during those early years of retirement. He was still the active partner, with many interests and hobbies, particularly gardening; she lived her life through his. Many were the times when he would spend a busy afternoon tending his plants, whilst she, motionless, watched him from the vantage point of her armchair.

In 1987 Sarah's worst fears were realised. She lost her father suddenly, in his mid-60s, and recognised that she alone carried the responsibility for a less than independent mother. Sarah was aston-ished to find that her mum seemed to be coping well in the immediate throes of bereavement, while she herself took the loss very badly. After six months or so, however, friends and neighbours in Amanda's village began to withdraw from providing the intensive support they had given in the immediate aftermath of Ted's death. They were beginning to perceive her as an encumbrance, as she transferred some of her previous dependence on her husband onto their shoulders. Her constant requests to accompany them on even short shopping expeditions were wearing them down, for instance.

It was at this stage that Amanda's mental health began to deteriorate rapidly. With her history of depression, she was very vulnerable to its advances and before long she had reached a very low ebb. Her depression, which was partly a response to her grief, was mixed with a good deal of anxiety, so that she became very agitated. The doctors prescribed the antidepressant drugs which had helped during her previous illness.

Sarah was faced with a difficult decision. How could she best care for her mum? Although Amanda only lived at the other side of London, in a Sussex village, the journey home took Sarah three hours, since she had no car. Her mum was close enough for a weekend visit, but too far away for Sarah to 'pop in' on from time to time to check she was managing. Sarah had to consider the possibility of moving down to Sussex.

It was difficult to know what to do for the best. It was not as if Amanda was a frail old lady. She was only in her mid-60s. Besides, she was reasonably capable in a physical sense. She has suffered a little from colitis, diverticulitis and pernicious anaemia, but even these complaints are felt by doctors to have psychological roots. Her dependency has been conditioned. For instance, she will not use buses, because her husband always drove her to the local shops, which means she relies on others for help with shopping. Amanda was looking to Sarah to step into her father's shoes, taking on the organisation of household affairs, but Sarah questioned whether it would be fair on her mum to give in to this pressure. Sarah believed, through faith in God, that even at 60-plus years of age, her mum was capable of change, despite what those around her said about the inevitability of Amanda's state of dependence.

Then there was the question of whether moving back home would have a beneficial effect on Amanda's health. Sarah seriously doubted whether her mother's health would significantly improve for having her daughter around the house more.

Sarah had her own needs to consider too. She had a rewarding, fulfilling job. Was it right for her to give it up to move close to her mum, when she could not guarantee finding another such position? She needed to support herself financially, in any case. Also, what effect would Amanda's state of mind have upon Sarah? Sarah was already returning from visits home in morose mood, feeling unable to muster the energy to go into work the following day. She feared that living with her mum would drive her into a state of mental instability.

Then there was the history of Sarah and Amanda's relationship to be borne in mind. As a little girl, Sarah had always felt more drawn to the charismatic, capable persona of her father, with whom she enjoyed a special friendship. Looking back, Sarah could see how this may have created some of the tensions that still exist between herself and her mother. A close, confiding relationship Sarah has known with neither of her parents, but she always felt a greater affinity with her father. She questioned whether now she would be able to change the course of her relationship with her mother. She admits she would never have sought out her mother as a friend, though she feels an obligation to support and care for her.

Sarah was forced to take a long, hard look at herself. Was she the caring, protective type who could cope with another person's dependency? She had always found difficulties in situations in her work and personal life when people around her became sick or too dependent upon her. She was definitely not 'maternal' by nature, she felt.

Sarah decided, for her mum's sake, and for her own, that she would maintain the status quo. She would continue to spend one weekend in every three or four with her mum and keep in telephone contact for the remainder of the time. She would try to liaise from her London base with medical professionals dealing with her mum.

In the early days, those weekends were gruelling for Sarah. Her visits became a constant battle between herself and her mother. Sarah insisted that Amanda help her with household tasks, resisting the pressure to take on the management of her mother's home. Amanda, for her part, became angry and frustrated, often screaming at Sarah to do things for her. After two years of persisting, Sarah has now managed to persuade her mum to help her out in the kitchen, when she visits, and to take on responsibility for her own domestic affairs. She has convinced her mum that she is no 'super-woman', that she cannot take on her father's role.

Progress has been slow, however. The antidepressant drugs have reduced Amanda's anxiety, but her life is dogged by an overwhelming sense of apathy, lethargy and hopelessness, even two years after she became depressed. Sarah finds obstacles that are all but insurmountable in motivating her mum to engage in any kind of activity. A kindly Christian lady in the village collects Amanda and gives her tea with her family once or twice each week. Friends take her shopping, the hairdresser calls once a week and she spends a day a week at the psychiatric day hospital, but, aside from these events, she does scarcely anything.

Sarah found out about a local MIND support group, for people with mental health problems. She gave her mum the details, but Amanda did nothing about it. Neither will she go to church anymore. The consequence is that Amanda takes no opportunity to meet and mix with new people. Her social circle is becoming ever narrower as she alienates friends and neighbours with her excessive demands, as Sarah sees it.

Similarly, when Sarah visits, she finds that her mum will sit doing nothing for much of her stay. It is only with considerable effort that she can persuade her mum to play Scrabble with her. This inactivity depresses Sarah, who is a person who likes to keep busy – reading, solving crossword puzzles etc.

Also frustrating for Sarah is Amanda's negative approach to life. She seems unable to 'count her blessings', in Sarah's estimation, focusing endlessly on all the negatives in her life. If there is something about which to complain, says Sarah, she will complain. She has never been seriously suicidal, according to the doctors who treat her, but has sometimes used the threat of suicide to manipulate, says Sarah.

In the two years since her mum was first ill, Sarah has seen a few signs of improvement in some areas, but these have often been offset by deterioration in others. She worries about the effects of the drugs on her mother's condition and is very frustrated that she must expend so much energy trying to contact medical staff who then often give the impression that they feel she is interfering.

It is a lonely and sad load of anxiety and stress that Sarah carries. She regrets that she has no brothers or sisters to help lighten the burden. She is fearful of her mum's neighbours. They have on occasions rung to complain bitterly of her mum's behaviour. Her mum went through a phase of screaming in her home to attract the neighbours' attention. They made recordings of the disturbance and threatened court action. They have made veiled accusations that

Sarah is failing in her responsibilities and have worn her down with their criticism.

Perhaps another source of loneliness for Sarah is the fact that she receives so little from her mother in terms of support. On one occasion, Sarah even expressed her sense of being unsupported. She said to her mum that it felt as though she had lost both her parents. It is not that her mum is not generous in financial terms. She even gave Sarah a gift towards the cost of moving house. Her neglect is an emotional one. For Sarah it seems as if she is the mature sensible one, while her mother acts like a child. Only the roles are not quite reversed, because Amanda does not like receiving instruction or reproof from her daughter.

Before moving to her new flat, Sarah attended a Baptist church in another part of London. Unfortunately, the church offered her very little support, because it was going through a time of change and upheaval. She felt as though she was having to put a lot of effort and energy into the church, at a time when she needed to be receiving. People at the church would assure her that they considered her their 'sister', but the kind of siblings she wanted were those who would share in caring practically for her mother.

In general terms, Sarah's feelings about caring for her mum are very mixed. There are moments when she feels deep compassion for her mum. She finds it sad that a woman in her 60s is still so dependent on others and she can understand how her mum feels there is so little to live for now her days of caring for others are over. At other times, however, Sarah is infuriated by the negativity, the unresponsiveness and the apathy that mark her mum's behaviour. In moments of frustration she has been known to shout at her mum, or even slap her hand, something which she always regrets afterwards. The many books Sarah has read on depression emphasise how important a patient and accepting attitude on the part of relatives of depressed people is. But nowhere do these books explain how the relative is supposed to keep their temper! Her outbreaks of anger alarm Sarah, because she has never been an angry person; they demonstrate to her the tension she is under.

In many ways the future looks grim for Amanda. Her negative responses have become entrenched. Attempts to shift them using cognitive therapy have failed, so the doctors despair of a cure and have fallen back on a regime of drug treatment which Sarah feels may even contribute to her mum's inability to concentrate. Amanda has an ever-dwindling circle of friends. Those who attempt to keep up an acquaintance with her are driven away by her constant moaning and her basic inability to make conversation. Amanda has come to accept her situation passively, though she feels no one understands or has been through an experience like hers. She enjoys almost nothing at all. She and Sarah have considered the possibility of sheltered accommodation, but, for the time being, she prefers to be in her own home. Somehow she needs to rediscover that life is worth living.

As for Sarah, she has found within herself resources for coping with the stresses and strains of her life. She freely admits that, had she not known there was a God working for good through her situation, she could never have coped. She has managed to convince her mum that, just because she is sick, does not mean that she has no responsibilities. Thus, her mum is now less manipulative and thoughtless in the way she speaks to Sarah. She fights for the belief that, through God, her mum, who is a Christian herself, can change and will change, though she knows it would be easier to be defeatist and not expect change. She still feels she made the correct decision in not moving back home, but this assurance does not keep at bay occasional feelings of guilt. Sometimes she wishes wistfully that history had happened differently, that it were her dad for whom she were caring, but she is nevertheless committed to her mum.

There is an element of defeatism in her approach to her mum. She no longer tries as hard to motivate her mum or to cheer her up. Her strategy instead is to keep life as normal as possible.

Sarah does not feel as though she is at the peak of her spiritual experience. She is particularly conscious of her weaknesses, but feels this makes her more aware of God's grace. She also feels she is now, as a result of caring for her mum, more tolerant of weakness in others and feels she would be better able to counsel those in need. Of Christian friends, she asks a sensitivity which knows how and when to express concern. She has found herself becoming annoyed with some people whose response to her accounts of her problems has been to offer well-meaning but unhelpful advice. Others have pushed the questions too far, when she would rather not talk, while a few have hurt her by not mentioning the situation at all.

Offering help to hurting carers

Sarah's story illustrates very well some of the unpleasant feelings which looking after a sick person can bring about. She often finds herself feeling low after spending weekends with her mum. She experiences anger over her mum's negativity and helplessness. The anger even causes her to hit her mum from time to time, but this gives her a tremendous sense of guilt. The guilt is exacerbated by the feeling that she is not doing enough for her mum. In addition, she worries constantly that her mum might not be coping.

There were certain ways in which the responses of Christian friends to Sarah's situation were unhelpful. Some were too absorbed in their own anxieties about the church to notice Sarah's problems. Others had different reasons for holding back, perhaps fearing they would be unable to cope with Sarah's pain. Those who were willing to broach the subject were not always sensitive to her mood. Some pushed the questions too far, others insisted on offering advice when what she needed was someone to listen.

Sometimes our fear that we will be unable to cope with another person's pain is legitimate. Were we to say something, we might stir up painful feelings in response to which we might be unable to offer comfort. We need, perhaps, if this is the case, to receive guidance on developing appropriate skills. We could read Michael Jacob's book *Swift to Hear*, in the SPCK New Library of Pastoral Care Series.(3) Also recommended is Gerard Egan's book *The Skilled Helper*.(4) Scripture Union's Training Unit have produced a useful Do-it-Yourself pack on learning helping skills.(5) Alternatively, the National Council of Voluntary Organisations, and a Christian organisation called the Acorn Trust run useful short courses.(6) For a longer, more thorough training course in counselling skills, consult the British Association for Counselling's Directory.(7)

The art which is essential in helping those going through painful feelings is the ability to empathise. This is the capacity to put oneself in the shoes of the sufferer, and to reflect accurately, through our words, the nature and intensity of the feelings they are experiencing. By reflecting the person's true feelings, we will encourage them to explore those feelings in greater depth.

If opening a conversation with a carer seems difficult, think about the following examples, taken from this chapter. Imagine that Sarah has explained that she feels torn, unable to decide whether or not to move closer to her mum. Perhaps you could offer the possibility of a conversation by saying: 'You sound anxious, would you like to talk about it?' If you were in conversation with Tom, who we met earlier in the chapter, he might explain that he can hardly bear to look at photos of Dot when she was younger. You could say, 'You must feel very sad; would you like to talk about that?' or 'How are you coping with the change?'

In each situation, we need to be sure that the questions we ask are designed not to benefit ourselves, or as a response to our own needs, but with the best interests of the carer in mind. We need to avoid questions which satisfy our curiosity, or echo our own pain for the person. Instead, the question should be aimed at inviting and enabling the carer to delve into their own feelings and find ways of coping.

Besides focusing on our own needs, rather than the carer's, another danger is that we will fail to identify the true shape of the carer's feelings. We will, perhaps, underestimate – or even overestimate – their anxiety or grief and cause them to feel frustrated by our responses.

There are three golden rules in helping carers going through painful feelings: try not to judge the person; avoid giving advice; and steer away from being partisan. It is tempting to feel repulsed by feelings of strong anger. Similarly, we can easily attach blame to people who are depressed. These judgmental attitudes need to be avoided in helping carers. It is more than likely that the carer already has a strong sense that their anger is somehow wrong, and we should avoid heaping further guilt on them. Our acceptance and love should be unconditional, thus mirroring the love God feels for every carer.

Sarah became frustrated with some of her Christian friends because they continually pressed advice upon her. Often the advice was patently inappropriate and, in any case, she felt too tired and demoralised to put any of it into practice. What she did need were friends who were able to help her explore in her own mind the solutions to her dilemmas which best suited her mum and herself. When we recognise that we are not in a position to make choices which affect the lives of our caring friends, we will be better placed to help them make their own decisions.

Finally, we need to avoid taking sides. I found myself easily slipping into the trap, when talking to Sarah, of disapproving of her mum, Amanda. We need to remember that we hear about only one side of any caring relationship. Instead of commenting on the actions of the disabled person (or Tom's apparently negligent GP, to take another example), we should pursue the carer's own feelings about their situation.

Besides offering a listening ear, there are indirect ways in which we can help relieve the emotional pressures carers suffer. We can identify factors which exacerbate low moods and irritable tempers and seek to alleviate them. For instance, we can help reduce the exhaustion which carers endure, and which reduces their ability to cope, by offering them opportunities to take time away from caring (see chapter 5) and by giving practical help (see chapter 6). Also, small gestures of affection – baking a cake, taking round some flowers, sending a card with an encouraging message – can all help to lighten spirits and to affirm the carer.

Chapters 3 and 4 will build upon the information given in this chapter. In chapter 3, we will see how many of the carers' negative feelings also have a spiritual dimension. In chapter 4, we can see how negative emotions are caused by, or add to, relationship problems carers face.

References

1. Sara Tomlin, *Abuse of Elderly People: An Unnecessary and Preventable Problem*, British Geriatrics Society, 1989.
2. Virginia Alison and Fay Wright, *Still Caring*, Spastics Society, 1990.
3. Michael Jacobs, *Swift to Hear: Facilitating Skills in Listening and Responding*, SPCK New Library of Pastoral Care Series, 1985.
4. Gerard Egan, *The Skilled Helper: Model, Skills and Methods for Effective Helping*, Brooks/Cole, 1982 edition.
5. Do-it-Yourself Pack, *Christian Caring; A Do-it-Yourself Training Course in Helping Skills*, Scripture Union Training Unit (available from SU Training Unit, 26–30 Heathcoat Street, Nottingham NG1 3AA, 0602 418144), 1989.
6. National Council for Voluntary Organisations, 26 Bedford Square, London WC1B 3HU, 071 636 4066.
The Acorn Christian Healing Trust, Whitehill Chase, High Street, Bordon, Hampshire GU35 0AP, 0420 478121/472779.
7. British Association for Counselling, 1 Regent Place, Rugby, Warwickshire CV21 2PJ, 0788 578328.

3. Where is God in all this?

Life for Gwen and her family had not really been tinged with sadness until about four years ago. The two teenage girls, Jessica, 16, and Nicola, 14, and five-year-old twins, Alison and Cathy, were, or so their parents believed, healthy and happy children, living normal lives. Normal, that is, apart from one mysterious problem.

Nicola, Gwen and Tom's second child, had, since she was five, encountered problems walking. Also, sometimes, when swimming or playing on a swing, her arms would lock. Out walking, she would ask for frequent rests. The family attributed these problems, at least partially, to a lazy streak. Nonetheless, they were sufficiently anxious to take Nicola along to their GP and he diligently referred her to a number of specialists to establish the cause of the problem. Each time, the consultants found nothing amiss.

By the time Nicola reached the age of 14, her GP decided there might be some value in sending her to a private physiotherapist for some exercises. This physio was the first person to have some idea as to what might be the root of the problem. Once again, parents and daughter found themselves in a hospital waiting room. They were ushered in to see consultant number six, fully expecting the diagnosis they had always been given: 'You have here a child who wants to avoid games at school.'

Nothing could have prepared them for the shattering news they were to hear that day. Nicola, they were told, had been born with a rare strain of muscular dystrophy, in which symptoms usually only appeared in girls after the age of 21. One day she would be in a wheelchair. As Nicola dressed herself, the doctor gave the dazed parents as many details as he could, keeping from them none of the harsh facts of this destructive disease. Not only was their second daughter a victim, but their other three children could fall prey to it in the future.

Grasping at normality, and stalling for time, Tom and Gwen managed a trip to the supermarket. On their return home they were faced with the grim task of revealing to the other children as many of the details as they felt each could handle, and also of filling Nicola herself in on some of the information they had been given. It was not like having a baby, which followed several months of mental and practical preparation. Here were Gwen and Tom, themselves in stunned shock, having to reassure each of their children and adjust to a new lifestyle of what was to be an endless succession of medical appointments for Nicola. At that stage, Gwen and Tom did not have the heart to tell Nicola she was likely to be in a wheelchair within the next few years. In fact, the young girl seemed relieved to know the source of her health problems, having feared that she would die within weeks.

Nicola did not feel ready to tell other people about the diagnosis. So for two whole years, the only ones who shared the awful knowledge of the illness with the family were Gwen's parents (Gwen had been due to visit them the day after the diagnosis was made, and could not conceal from them her grief and anxiety), the family's vicar and four close friends.

Gwen carried an enormous strain. She felt all the sense of loss, fear and bewilderment any parent goes through when a child is found to be suffering from a serious incurable illness. But at the same time she felt the need to conceal her pain. She hid it from Nicola, so that their relationship became strained, based on a polite dishonesty. She felt so sorry for Nicola, and yet did not have the skills to know how to talk to her. She felt she must remain bright and cheerful, so that Nicola did not suspect that things were even worse than she had been told. But the mutual protectiveness they conspired to sustain placed a ghastly veneer on their relationship. Neither did Gwen dare show to the other children how deep were her fears about Nicola. Finally, she could not reveal to people outside the family that something was badly wrong.

How desperately Gwen needed those four friends. Many were the times when the distraught mother turned up on their doorsteps in a distressed frame of mind and received sympathy and comfort. Many were the times when these kind friends would step in to look after the twins while Gwen and Nicola visited the hospital. The Samaritans turned out to be trusted friends too. During those early months, Gwen went through all the stages that characterise grief, though she did not realise it at the time. She sometimes felt as if she was going mad.

Her faith meant a lot to Gwen, though. She had been a Christian for over 10 years, which persuaded her to believe that God would heal Nicola. All around her, in sermons, books and conversation with other Christians, seemed to be pointers to God's ability to heal the sick. If God could heal, he would heal her precious child. One night Gwen felt an uncharacteristic urge to lay hands on Nicola and pray for her healing while she slept. As she did so, she noticed Nicola's room was unusually warm for a chill winter night. She went next door to the twins' room and, noticing how much colder it felt, she took this strange occurrence as a sign that God would heal Nicola.

Gwen was horrified and perplexed when, a short while after this incident, Nicola's health took a turn for the worse. She descended from one of the plateaux which hold muscular dystrophy sufferers in a stable condition for periods, and there was a marked deterioration in her health. With this deterioration in Nicola's health came a crisis in Gwen's faith. How could a loving God be deaf to her anguished cries for her suffering child? She began to feel very angry with God.

There have been moments when Gwen has wanted to tear her Bible to pieces and put it in the dustbin. It would be so much easier if God healed no one. It would be more bearable if insensitive Christians ceased drawing Nicola's attention to healing miracles in the Bible. Christians who insisted on reassuring Gwen that 'this life is not important' failed to understand the heartache she endured each week as she witnessed the suffering of so many children at the hydro-therapy pool where Nicola was a patient. She hopes that someday her relationship with God will be mended, but for now she has 'stuffed him in a cardboard box' until she feels stronger.

When two years had elapsed since the diagnosis of the illness, Nicola entered the 6th form at school. Her doctors felt it was time she opened up about her illness. Only then could she receive the help she needed at school and around the village. In any case, her problems in walking were beginning to look obvious.

Nicola and Gwen felt a measure of relief when they decided to tell Nicola's school, through the headmaster, about her condition. The four friends who knew already agreed to ring round people in the congregation at church. At least now, thought Gwen, I shall not feel as if I am coping in isolation. We shall all be given moral support, Nicola from her schoolmates, Tom and I from friends at church.

Her hopes were shattered. The encouraging notes of sympathy, the phone calls of commiseration, never materialised. The family felt as though they were in a goldfish bowl, constantly being watched, but that no one cared enough to show it. Some longstanding friends of Gwen's have not to this day talked to her about Nicola. 'How's Jessica? How are the twins?' they ask. But never, 'How's Nicola?' It was almost as if Nicola were dead.

This practice of ignoring Nicola in conversation, which so many friends and acquaintances have adopted, has cut Gwen to the heart. It was yet another evidence of God's callousness. In the absence of the anticipated support, Gwen was left again relying on the kindness of her original four comforters.

If the end of the first two years marked any improvement, it was in Gwen's relationship with her daughter. They were once again able to share a deep, honest friendship. They spent many a happy hour talking together, particularly about the people they know. Nicola has a deep trust in God, which sustains her, and has become neither bitter nor resentful. Gwen still feels a deep sorrow for her child, though. Nicola has now left home to study, but returns home most weekends.

Although, four years after her diagnosis, she is still not in a wheelchair, she cannot trust her legs. They are liable to give way under her, sending her crashing to the floor. She is slight, so falls cause her intense pain, not to mention the risk of broken bones which could cause her condition to deteriorate rapidly because of the restrictions it would place upon exercise. When Nicola falls, the pain she suffers makes it difficult to lift her, a situation Gwen cannot bear to witness. Nicola generally finds she cannot pick up things she drops either, or get up from a table without extreme difficulty. Now she is away studying, Gwen cannot understand where she found the time to continually chauffeur her daughter around the village and to hospital appointments.

Gwen has learned to live with the hurtful responses of Christian friends. Counselling has helped her to understand the insecurity which lies behind the insensitive reactions of those around her. An experience with one of the twins' school teachers, Mrs Clark, showed Gwen why people had been avoiding her. Mrs Clark had been a teacher of Nicola's and had been devastated to hear of the girl's illness. She promised Gwen that she would come round to talk, but she never came. Later, when the twins' schooling required Gwen to visit Mrs Clark, the teacher asked, 'How's Nicola?' And she began to cry. She explained that tears were shed in the staff-room each time Nicola's name was mentioned, but no one knew what to say to Gwen, and so they had retreated into silence. Mrs Clark admitted she could never face hearing what Gwen would tell her about Nicola, so she stayed away from the family home. This frank, penitent confession began Gwen on the road towards understanding why those around her had not always offered support.

Gwen perceives other causes for the reticence she experienced in others. Had a relative been dying, Gwen suspects that neighbours and friends would have rallied round to offer help. But Nicola's is a chronic illness. The care she will need is long-term, and those who could help do not because they fear the implications of such a potentially long-term commitment.

Gwen feels strongly that the people who offered the most appreciated help were those who did not offer advice, or theological reasoning, but were prepared to stand alongside her in her grief and anger. They were the few who listened while she raged, accepted all her mixed emotions and, perhaps most importantly, shed sincere tears with her. They were those who were also practical in their thoughtfulness, offering to babysit for the family.

The future looks bleak to Gwen, but she is reaching a measure of acceptance, a realism. At times the problems overwhelm her, but she has found many opportunities to offer consolation to other distressed parents, despite her own pain. She has also, in the past, offered her services to the pastoral care team of the parish church to which she belongs, visiting lonely older people.

The other three children have all been affected by Nicola's illness in different ways. Alison, one of the twins, realised only months ago the full implications of Nicola's disability. Since then, she has shown many of the signs of depression, threatening on occasions to jump from her bedroom window. She is hypersensitive to the ways in which disabled people are treated and will become angry with her mother if she feels Gwen is making fun of people in wheelchairs. While Alison feels grief-stricken for her sister, however, there is also an element of jealousy in response to the extra attention Nicola's illness brings her.

Gwen speaks harshly about her eldest daughter, Jessica's, response to Nicola. Jessica, like Alison, feels a certain jealousy towards Nicola. She will, therefore, refuse to pick up things Nicola has dropped, and shout and swear at her. But she too will often cry when Gwen talks to her about Nicola. Obviously all three sisters have been affected in different ways, and the difficulties Tom and Gwen face in their role as parents are compounded by the individual responses of each. None of the three show signs of developing muscular dystrophy, but living with the fear of such a possibility must be hard to bear.

Gwen very much hopes she will one day rediscover the deep peace which she believes Christianity is all about, a peace unswayed by outward circumstances. She is still very angry with God, but there is a thread of hope that she will see God again through the pain.

Meeting Gwen was for me, at one and the same time, a powerful, and yet a disturbing, encounter. Here was a woman whose faith, or so she thought, had been invulnerable, until an experience of great suffering blew against and through it a wind of great change. It was an experience for me which evoked spiritual humility, a sense that we all face the danger that pain will turn us against our God. It called me to reaffirm the belief that, no matter how distant we feel from God, he remains close.

What went wrong?

It seems that several factors contributed to the demise of Gwen's spiritual confidence. At the root of her crisis was, I believe, a theological misunderstanding. In a culture where scientific progress has cushioned us against the blows life inflicted on our predecessors, and still inflicts on peoples the world over, we have come to expect a suffering-free existence. This expectation spills over into the spiritual dimension of our lives. We are sold a Gospel that will free us from the distasteful side of life and offer joy and peace in its place. We peddle a sugary sweet God of love who exists to rescue us from the unpleasant. We measure our spiritual progress against a yardstick of how well we cope with life. To struggle is to fail.

None of this prepares us for the intense pain to which, as frail human beings, we are still prone. God is no longer solving my problems, so how can he be a God of love? This is the predominant spiritual sensation of all those who have suffered, like myself, from the gruelling experience of depressive illness. This was precisely Gwen's dilemma. Taught to expect success and victory over pain, she was not equipped to meet with endurance one of the most painful experiences life could have dealt her. Worse still, her past life as a Christian had led her to believe in only one solution as acceptable, that of supernatural healing.

Gwen's response was not unusual. How many, faced with the agony and futility of suffering, do not pose the question 'Why?' Theologians from different traditions have grappled with the issue for centuries. Many reason that, without suffering, growth is impossible. Others even say that God himself, through the cross, was changed by the suffering of Christ.(1) An answer to the question of suffering which satisfies those undergoing torment will never be found this side of heaven, but teaching which excludes suffering from the scope of the Christian faith, fails to prepare adequately Christians who suffer, and treats as inferior those already mortified by physical and mental anguish.

Gwen had no past memories of suffering with which to compare this new agony, but neither had she been taught to expect and embrace suffering as part of Christianity. She was, therefore, puzzled and angry with God. Doubtless, had she been adequately prepared, she would still have raged against God, but at least some of the dissonance between her present situation and her previous expectations would have been reduced.

Part of the anger directed at God however was, at root, a response, not to God himself, but to the mediators of his love, the Christians around Gwen. So many of them were unhelpful in their response. There was the silence of those whose pain prevented them from reaching out to Gwen. There was the insensitivity of those who persisted in offering homilies, detailing the spiritual lessons to be learned, piously, as Job's comforters, uttering words of wisdom which failed to harmonise with Gwen's bruised feelings.

What helped? Some lessons

Having considered the unhelpful elements of Gwen's experiences, we can now pick up on a few positives. Several friends were willing to stand alongside, to enter into the suffering, to cry with Gwen, and to listen without judging as she poured out her soul. These were the friends who knew not to offer hollow theological explanations.

What lessons are to be learned from Gwen's experiences? Firstly, we can see how important it is to have thought through our own suffering theology and then to know when to share it with those around us who suffer. Otherwise, the danger is that we ourselves will be sucked into the crisis of the sufferer. Witnessing the pain of others can easily cause us to question the love of God, at a moment when the sufferer perhaps needs to know that our own faith is secure. We need, consequently, to be sure in our own minds about the role suffering can play in the Christian life. Whilst never welcoming it, we can affirm the spiritual integrity of those enduring it. Any Christian bookshop will hold a number of useful books on suffering. Some, like Joni Eareekson Tada's *Glorious Intruder*, are autobiographical. Other's, like Lord Longford's book *Suffering and Hope*, look at the topic more broadly.(2)

A second lesson I needed to learn from my meeting with Gwen was that I was not seeing her life in its entirety. I met her at a moment when she had reached a very low spiritual ebb. I could so easily have despaired of her ever finding her way back to God. I had to trust that her Heavenly Father had Gwen in his hands and was leading her through this painful stage towards greater oneness with him. Gwen herself had a faint sense of this. I needed to believe that God would gently guide her through the minefield of suffering, that the deep truths he was teaching were ones I could not understand. I had to relinquish my strong urge to transfer my faith to her, to offer platitudes, and to rest instead in the belief that God, in his perfect time, would reveal these things to her.

Thirdly, Gwen's story reinforces the need for helpers to be prepared to listen without judging. Those who helped most were those with whom she could share her deepest resentments and anxieties. They had time and the discipline to remain still and quiet, respecting the sentiments expressed uncensoriously. They also saw that to offer advice or attempt to impose solutions to the problem would be unwise. Chapter 2 offers some advice on developing skills in helping others through listening. We need to cultivate the art of listening in an age when many voices compete for attention.

Fourthly, Gwen considered as a great privilege the willingness of close friends simply to 'be with' her through the darkness. Do we seriously believe that we can offer effective support if we are unable to shed sincere tears with those who weep? If we do, how well are we reflecting the tenderness of our Lord whose heart was moved to tears by the distress of his bereaved friends, Mary and Martha (John 11:32–35)? I suspect that Gwen's friends found their empathy did not sit comfortably on their shoulders. It hurts to put yourself in the shoes of someone enduring hardship. It is much easier to take the route of the majority of Gwen's friends, avoiding the sufferer. Ultimately, if we are to follow the path of Christ, the people with whom we choose to spend time will include the sick and their families. 'Being with' the sick is part of what distinguishes the sheep from the goats in Jesus' parable (Matthew 25:36).

Caring: The spiritual dimension

It would be inaccurate to suggest that, in spiritual terms, carers differ from the rest of us. In many senses, their needs are the same as those of any Christian. They require spiritual food and fellowship to flourish, as do the rest of us. In some respects, however, caring generates intense spiritual yearnings to which the Church, in its pastoral care, and we as individuals, must address ourselves.

Much of the secular research literature focuses on aspects of the caring role as problems with feelings. Anyone attending a meeting at which a group of carers is present cannot fail to notice these feelings. The many tears which are shed reveal how close to the surface streams a well of relentless grief, anger and despair. These tears shock, when one considers the reluctance with which we British cry publicly. In the previous chapter, we described some of the tear-inducing feelings. Looked at closely, we find, however, that many of them are in fact part of a person's spiritual response to human tragedy. They can be alleviated on the emotional level, but for some carers the spiritual dimension must also be explored.

We saw in chapter 2 how many carers live in a state of perpetual anxiety. The uncertainty of not knowing what the future holds can be intolerable. There is the worry that one might, at some stage, be unable to continue caring. Also, the troubled heart restlessly ponders the quality of the care it gives, looking for areas for self-reproach. For the Christian carer, this anxiety can be accentuated, because it is translated into the spiritual realm, causing doubt, the suspicion that God is not in control, or worse, non-existent.

Anxiety can be tackled in very practical ways. Modern psychiatry has developed effective 'anxiety management' techniques, foremost among which is helping the sufferer to learn how to relax. Revd Michael Wright has researched the experience of stress amongst carers and developed a programme for helping them counteract it.(3) He has also discovered that, for many carers, faith has enabled them to confront their anxieties.

Like all Christians experiencing spiritual crisis, carers need affirmation and patience. They certainly do not need to have additional guilt heaped upon them by those who cannot cope with their doubt. They need to be able to talk through their doubts. They need to know that the questions are legitimate and that God has allowed his followers to ask them throughout history and even used them to establish a closer bond with his children.

We saw in chapter 2 how, very often, carers experience great sadness. Many, like Gwen, go through an experience akin to bereavement, grieving over shattered dreams, the loss of a healthy child, spouse or parent, yearning for the life that was. It is excruciatingly painful to see a loved one afflicted with debilitating illness. As helpers we need to remember just how jarring, in spiritual terms, this can be. All around them the carer sees Christians, surrounded by smiling families, apparently coping with life cheerfully, even joyfully. The Bible is full of injunctions to 'rejoice always'. A sprinkling of guilt is then added to a veritable stew of defeated dolefulness to produce an unedifying spiritual diet for the carer.

To greet this sorrow with flippant protestations of, 'Cheer up!

It's not that bad really,' is evidently inappropriate. How could we ever know how bad it is? We need to listen carefully in order to reflect back to the carer the true nature and intensity of what they are feeling. Perhaps we need to accept the sad person, whilst refusing to accept the sadness. Carers need to know that it is not 'unchristian' to feel sad. They need to be able to talk frankly about their grief with fellow-Christians without fear of judgment. But they also need help in overcoming the sadness wherever possible.

A steady, caring friendship can go a long way towards alleviating some of the sadness. Such friendship feeds the spirit and soul of a carer. A true friend will know how and at what moment to encourage a carer to look for some of the positives, some of the evidence of God's continued provision and goodness. If sadness persists over a long period, interfering in the carer's spiritual life and preventing them from relating to others, a good friend will persist in encouraging the carer to enlist the help of someone skilled in working with those who are low in spirit, be that person a Christian minister, a counsellor or a doctor.

However caring a Christian friend may be, they need to acknowledge that their skills are not unlimited, that sometimes others may need to be called upon to help. There may come a time when, thankful though they are for your continuing support, a carer needs extra help in working through a specific problem, or in exploring some aspect of their feelings. In this event, you might be in a position to suggest that they speak to a trained counsellor, for instance, or pay a visit to their local office of Relate (formerly the Marriage Guidance Council). Only with this specialist help may some of the 'joy of the Lord' return to the carer.

Many carers, as we saw in chapter 2, are angry. They are angry with the sick person because of their constant demands, angry with relatives who refuse to help, angry with unhelpful professionals. In this chapter, we need to recognise that many carers are, like Gwen, angry with God. Some carers literally feel that God has played a trick on them. He has rewarded their faith with an experience of great pain. He has the power, or so they believe, to transform the situation, but he is passive. It is almost as though God has stolen from them something precious and they determine to rage until he returns it.

It is often difficult to know what to say and how to react when faced with this anger. To an observer, it can appear ugly. It can also disturb the easy equilibrium of our day-to-day walk with God. Whatever else we say or do, it would be damaging to ask carers to suppress their anger towards God. Anger turned in on itself, as psychologists tell us, can easily become self-destructive depression. We have somehow to find a way to acknowledge and accept the anger as valid, without fuelling it. The best way of doing this is to avoid either underestimating it or overplaying it in the responses we make.

It may seem that anger towards God is disrespectful, but you need only glance at the Psalms to realise that Biblical characters had no reservations about blaming God for their misfortunes. Perhaps we should help carers to realise that, since they cannot conceal their fury from God, it might be of use to express it honestly before him and, thereby, at least engage in dialogue with him, however heated! At the same time as offering empathy and understanding (who would not feel angry at a God who allowed a loved one to be struck down by disease?) we must avoid feeding the carer's frustrations by failing to acknowledge them adequately.

We saw in chapter 2 how carers often feel guilty for feeling anger towards a person who is frail and sick. Of all the problems carers face, surely the Church has an answer to this one. The Christian faith revolves around the existence of human guilt and offers a solution to it. Christianity does not condone black emotions, such as resentment or misplaced anger. But neither does it allow its followers to be paralysed by guilt induced by them. It reveals that, through the sacrifice made on the cross, the burden of guilt we each carry can be removed. Resentment and bitterness are not constructive emotions. They lead carers to feel unhappy with themselves. Surely it is more helpful to suggest a solution to them, than merely to offer sympathetic nods? To know that in Jesus there is cleansing and forgiveness can be a source of comfort to carers and is a truth of which they can be reminded.

You will see from the story of Brenda, later in this chapter, that coming face to face with our own selfishness, through having to put the needs of another person first, can be useful. It enables some carers to see their own weakness and their need for God's mercy and to understand those around them who sin when faced with external pressures.

There is some guilt in caring which is misplaced, however. Carers frequently feel that their caring is inadequate, no matter to what lengths they push themselves. For those with disabled children, the guilt is compounded by the notion that somehow one is to blame for one's child's disability. This self-recrimination must be confronted, because it is damaging and patently false. We need to reassure carers that their resources are not limitless and that there is only a certain level of care which they can be expected to give. Unfortunately, it is the deficiencies in support from the state, amongst other sources, that leave carers feeling it is their duty to do everything. Secondly, we must challenge the belief that the carer is in some way to blame for their relative's suffering.

Some aspects of the problems carers face in relationships, which we will consider in chapter 4, have a spiritual demension too. The loneliness many feel spills over into their inner lives, so that they feel isolated from the Christian community. It seems that no one can fully understand or enter into the spiritual issues which trouble them. Some feel never more abandoned than when in church, surrounded by people who seem to have not a clue what caring is all about.

How to help

We have already begun to see that, as Christians, we can offer something positive to carers. We can respond to them as if we believe that God's 'glory' can be in the midst of suffering, working for good even in apparently hopeless situations.

Much of helping carers face spiritual crises is about approach, as we saw in the last section. It is about accepting and loving them, no matter what the doubts, how intense the anger, how deep the sadness. It is about listening and working with carers, as they resolve some of the issues. It is certainly not about giving advice. Helping carers negotiate spiritual crises *is* about keeping them regularly and faithfully in our prayers. Letting them know that we pray for them is also beneficial. There are, however, rather more practical ways in which we can go about helping with the spiritual issues arising from caring. These types of helping fall into two categories: the help which enables carers to enjoy the same benefits of church life that the rest of us take for granted; and the help which takes into account their special needs.

We remarked earlier in the chapter upon the fact that carers have the same needs as all Christians. They need to feel part of a Christian community. They will flourish only when provided with the nourishment which makes up the spiritual diet of the average Christian involved in a local church. But for carers, having these basic spiritual needs met can prove impossible.

Speaking recently to an official of a carers support group, I was appalled to learn that three out of every four members had past connections with local churches. Each had dropped out of church life as a result of the pressures they faced. Some found their churches did not offer a welcome, in physical or social terms, to their disabled relative. For those whose relative was either unable, or not inclined, to go to church, finding a volunteer to sit with them during services had not been possible. Sadly, their disappearance from church life was scarcely noticed, and it was assumed that they had chosen to distance themselves from church life out of preference.

As the friend of a Christian carer, there are many things we can do to avoid this situation. One of the most obvious steps we can take is to offer directly to sit with the disabled person on the occasional Sunday, thus freeing the carer to go to church. It would probably be helpful to specify how frequently you would be willing to do this, so that your carer friend does not feel embarrassed about asking.

On the other hand, if the disabled person would like to go to church with their carer, a different approach is needed. It is helpful to ensure that the carer feels that they and their relative are welcome in the church. How sad it is that many disabled people feel marginalised and ignored in church, so that their carer feels reluctant to subject them to church services very often. Much of this rebuff stems from the unfriendly physical structures of a church building. Access for wheelchairs is poor in many churches and accommodating them difficult, so that the disabled person is embarrassingly placed in an aisle or, conspicuously, at the front of the church. As individuals we must support organisations like Church Action on Disability which are campaigning for better church facilities for disabled people.(4) But as individuals too we can help to make changes like these a priority for our churches.

Giving a welcome to disabled people involves far more than adapting buildings, however.(5) Only when attitudes are accepting and bridges built between the able-bodied and physically and mentally disabled communities, will disabled people, and in turn their relatives, feel truly at home in our churches.(6)

We need to notice when carers do not come on Sundays and take the time to find out the reasons behind their absence. If a temporary crisis, or longer term circumstances, prevent them from attending services, there are ways in which we can continue to help the carer feel part of the church. We can tape sermons, deliver church notice sheets, pop in from time to time to discuss church news.

Many carers continue to desire to contribute actively to the life of the church, so that creative ways of maintaining their role have to be found by each of us as individual Christians. It can be hurtful when others assume that, because the carer's life has become more home-based, the only feasible part they can play in church life is in baking cakes for church events. To continue as church secretary, as worship leader, as Sunday School teacher, might be one way in which a carer maintains vital links with life outside their home. To offer help in facilitating these functions is much appreciated.

These are all ways in which carers can be helped by individuals in their churches to maintain their role in church life. The following suggestions, however, are designed to help in offering the special and unique spiritual help that carers need.

It is important not to make assumptions about the situation each carer faces. It will vary according to their position in the family – what relationship they bear to the person they are looking after and the proximity of other relatives, for instance. It will be affected by the nature and level of the disability their relative suffers. It will be partially determined by the personality and individual response of the carer. And it will change over time. This means that the carer's role in their church needs to be continually monitored and re-assessed. What might be an appropriate level of commitment in the early stages of caring, may not be feasible as time goes on. Later in this chapter we will see how Brenda's church fellowship failed to talk through with her the contribution she was able to make to the pastoral care it offered, once she had undertaken to care at home for her mother. It is important to maintain dialogue with the carer, and to give them permission to adjust their role in church life as circumstances dictate.

It is unfortunate that, at a stage in their lives of frequently heightened spiritual need, carers often lack access to the help that would see them through spiritual crises. The caring role absorbs so much time and energy, that tending to one's own needs, least of all one's spiritual needs, can prove difficult. Rather than having to seek out spiritual assistance, perhaps that assistance could be taken to them. Those in the church with pastoral and counselling gifts have an obvious role to play and could offer to visit the carer and sensitively talk through some of the spiritual issues with which they are grappling. For those lacking specific gifts in this area, simply to listen helps a lot. One carer I spoke to recently mentioned affectionately the retired clergyman whose timely and wise words helped her to come to terms with her child's severe disability.

There might be a case for initiating some kind of informal Bible study group for carers in your congregation which took account of the need to make arrangements for providing for their disabled relatives during meetings. Merely introducing Christian carers to one another can help reduce some of the spiritual isolation.

A final idea for helping carers concerns the common lack of space for contemplation. The demands of caring often squeeze out time for quietness and meditation. Spiritual crises can go unresolved for many years for want of time to reflect. I feel that we could do many carers a favour if we allowed them time to retreat from the relentless challenges of day to day life and to recharge physical, spiritual and emotional batteries. For centuries, members of religious orders have offered the solace of quietness and unobtrusive kindness within their own communities to the world weary. Surely this is a service from which many carers could benefit? Information about retreat centres is readily available through the National Retreat Association.(7) I feel it could be very helpful to offer information about local retreat centres to carers in our churches, volunteering hospitality for their disabled relative, should they want to get away at any stage.

The following story of the spiritual journey of a carer offers more hope than the account of Gwen's life given earlier in this chapter. From it can be drawn the conclusion that caring can deepen a person's faith and bring them a greater sensitivity to the needs of those around them, a truer conception of self.

The first thing you notice when you meet Brenda is her warmth. She is now in her early 40s and enjoys helping those around her in the dilemmas they face. Whenever she can, she gives of her time, her energy, her home, to comfort and counsel those in need.

I found that Brenda was incisively perceptive, able to interpret and articulate human emotion with ease. Not only can she empathise, but she has a rare depth of compassion and integrity which reassures those who speak to her that their confidence is safe with her. Her relationships with those close to her speak of this kindness. She is linked with a strong bond to her husband, Dave, though their relationship has known the low points which most marriages experience. Though she is sad that neither of her daughters, Janet, 21, and Emma, 19, feel the Christian faith has much relevance to them at this stage in their lives, she is able to relate to them in a deep and satisfying way. She is separated by only a couple of years from her younger sister, Jenny, and a lot of affection flows between the two.

Considering the strength of Brenda's relationships with most of her loved ones, it is strange to contemplate the emotional distance which has separated her from her mum, Lilian, for many years now. But this distance was never of Brenda's choosing.

Lilian's story evokes immediate sympathy. It seems that life has been cruel in the blows it has dealt her. Her experience of parenthood has been tinged with grief, for her first child died as a baby. Death has also taken three husbands from her before she reached her 60s. Neither has she enjoyed good health. A weak heart has been her lot for many years. It was in 1989, however, that she was brought low with life-threatening illness. She suffered a massive stroke and was given only a few days to live. Miraculously she pulled through, but doctors expected her never to regain her speech and to need full-time professional care for the rest of her life.

Her present state of health is testimony to her own courage and the determination, love and prayers of the people who care about her. Lilian's main problem now is one of co-ordination. It means she needs help in walking, in particular. She can just about feed herself and has miraculously recovered her speech. She says she is being punished for the wild life she has lived, which, reports Brenda, could have been a response to the strict Baptist upbringing she had. It has been at moments of loss that Lilian has turned for support to her children. When she lost her husbands, she felt unable to manage alone and, on the last two occasions, moved in with Brenda and Dave for a while. Excluding these troubled times, however, she has been self-reliant. She has tended to engross herself in the social milieux of each husband, so has seen little of Brenda, her other daughter Jenny, and her son Michael, during their adulthood.

Brenda recounts fondly that Lilian has always been capable of compelling the attention of those around her. She is accustomed to being noticed in a crowd and likes to be at the centre of social activity. She wants to be 'everything' to those with whom she spends each part of her life.

Once the initial turmoil of those few agonising days after the stroke was over, and there were signs of marked improvement, the family together began to consider the future. As Lilian's condition became progressively better, professionals involved also joined in discussions about what would happen to her next. Michael, Lilian's son, found the experience of witnessing his mum's illness too traumatic to be prepared to take her into his home. Jenny, her younger daughter, had recently given birth to her seventh child and therefore had neither time nor energy to devote to looking after a frail old lady.

As for Brenda's situation, that was far from ideal, as the family home had a bathroom and toilet only on the first floor and Lilian could not manage stairs. In the end, it was decided that Brenda was in the best position to take on caring for her mum, a commode was found, and Lilian moved in. The room at the front of the house downstairs was turned into a bed-sit for her. Michael has continued to have very little involvement in the situation, but Jenny has become more active, although she has provided emotional support to Brenda throughout.

Adjusting to living so closely together was easy for neither Brenda nor Lilian. It imposed a level of intimacy they had never known. For Lilian, it was embarrassing to need so much help from her daughter in the basic tasks of living, such as getting up in the morning, and going to the toilet throughout the day. For Brenda, it was like having young children again, only without the physical stamina. There was always someone in the house for whose care she was responsible. Spending time with her husband, Dave, presented enormous obstacles. Contrary to what she had expected, Brenda coped much better with the nursing tasks she had to perform than with the new restrictions on her life.

Although Brenda has not been in paid work since her children were born, she and Dave are involved in the leadership of the Christian Fellowship to which they belong. They also spend much time counselling folk who are linked to the fellowship, feeling God has called them to this ministry. Prior to her stroke, Lilian was scarcely aware of the many people who came to her daughter's home for relief from their anxieties. When she came to live with her, however, it was something she learned to resent. It was a call upon Brenda's time and energy, depriving Lilian of her daughter's company and reminding her of her own loneliness. Here was proof that Brenda had a life and that she did not. Here was evidence that she, Lilian, was not 'everything' to her daughter, and it hurt.

Aware of her mum's feelings towards these counselling commitments, Brenda experienced a tremendous sense of conflicting loyalties. Her heart was drawn to the souls around her in emotional need, and yet she saw her mum's loneliness and diminishing self-confidence. If anyone's needs were left out, they were Brenda's own needs.

To compound the tensions, both women found difficulty relating to the other's God. Lilian's God is aloof and punishing, demanding holiness. Having grown up with similar images of God, Brenda has since discovered a more loving, approachable God. Brenda's expression of faith is, she says, 'charismatic' too, making her mum suspicious. With her experience in counselling, Brenda can see emotions in her mum that need to be resolved. In particular, she feels that Lilian has not grieved properly over her lost loved ones. Eager to reach out to her mum and offer solace, Brenda was disappointed to realise that the dynamics of their relationship precluded this.

On one occasion, Lilian opened up about her feelings over her lost child and the difficulty she had faced in accepting and loving Brenda, her second child. This was a precious moment for both, but one from which Lilian quickly retreated. There were a few opportunities for the two to pray together over their anguish at the frustrations of Lilian's disability, but mostly the older lady was not happy to open out to her daughter. Eventually Brenda came to accept this situation and to realise that, if help were to come, it were best received from Lilian's own church, to which Jenny, Brenda's sister, took her most weeks.

As the months passed, the tensions in Brenda's role became increasingly apparent and more and more intolerable. She managed, with great difficulty, to set aside time each day to pray over counselling situations and draw strength to continue. But Lilian was increasing the pressure upon her to drop commitments to church, while requests for help from church members did anything but diminish. In moments of intense frustration and exhaustion, Brenda found herself thinking that, if only her mother died, these conflicts would be resolved.

It was not that Brenda was unwilling to give herself over completely to caring for her mum. It was just that she had difficulty discerning God's purpose in the situation. The uncertainty of the future was not easy to bear. At the same time, Lilian was warming to the idea of moving into a home. The company and stimulation it would give was appealing. She began looking at homes with the family and found several pleasant. She was put on waiting lists for rooms, but Dave and Brenda put the possibility on one side, as waiting lists were very long.

One weekend a very demanding counselling case, which highlighted the conflicts, brought matters to a head. On Sunday evening Brenda cried out to God to show them his plan. Within hours the answer came. The very next morning the phone rang. It was someone from a nearby home, ringing to say that a place was available for Lilian. The next few days and weeks confirmed, in Brenda's mind, that the home was God's provision for Lilian. It was in a street close to where she and Dave lived. The atmosphere was friendly and Lilian, who was inclined to worry about health, felt secure, surrounded by medically qualified staff.

As time has gone on, Lilian has fitted very well into nursing home life. She has become protective towards other residents, sending Brenda on errands to buy sweets for them. As Brenda says, Lilian is as happy as she would be anywhere. She has many visitors, chief among whom are her two daughters, and many opportunities to get out. Her relationship with Brenda seems, if anything, improved, now there is less intimacy between them.

Reflecting upon her year's experience of caring, Brenda can see many things which God taught her through it. She was brought face to face with her own capacity to feel intense anger and resentment, making her more tolerant of those around her who are driven by circumstances to wrong words and actions. Having to serve another person so completely taught her much about her own instinctive selfishness. She feels she knows herself better as a result, and is also able to sympathise with other carers more deeply.

Like many who are tested to the limit, she can also testify to the irrational joy God can give regardless of a person's situation. At moments of frustration and anxiety it seemed that God would flood her heart with his peace. She feels, too, that she was called upon to exercise more trust than she had ever done before. It was tempting to worry about the future, but she learned to rest in God and take each day as it came. She feels for carers who have no faith to sustain them.

Several Christian friends were very helpful throughout the time spent caring. One, a social worker, advised the family of the financial benefits to which they were entitled. She also ensured that they took a break in her holiday cottage every eighth weekend, while Lilian went back into hospital, and even drove them there, since they had no car. Another friend, who works with carers, urged the couple to assess very carefully at the start whether or not they could cope with caring for Lilian, insisting that, should they decide to do so, Brenda maintain some of her own interests to preserve her identity.

Another friend and neighbour, who belonged to the fellowship and who had cared for her own mother with multiple sclerosis, listened while Brenda from time to time poured out her frustrations. Emma, Dave and Brenda's younger daughter, who was still living at home, was angry when her gran took over the front room of the house where she had entertained friends, but was willing to sit with her on occasions when Dave and Brenda wanted to go out together. Dave himself was a tower of strength. Though reserved by nature, he was a vehicle of compassion towards his mother-in-law, and an encourager to Brenda, insisting that they spend some time together each day to maintain their own closeness. Finally, Brenda and Lilian appreciated very much the visits they received regularly from a few members of Brenda and Dave's church.

Not everyone was as supportive as these people, though. Many in the church promised to visit Lilian, but failed to come, leading Brenda to feel that it is preferable to make no commitment than to make one and to fail to honour it. At the time when Lilian left hospital, many services were promised but few materialised, causing Brenda to feel that her ability to cope militated against her receiving help. Some of the services offered did not work out well, either, because Lilian rejected them, or because guidelines about their use were not given.

Though Brenda and Dave's fellowship seems to be caring and

warm, there was a lack of insight into the problems that caring at home can involve. Lilian's church seemed culpable on the surface. Lilian was rarely visited, but this, says Brenda, was largely because the church was located several bus rides away from their home and many of the members were elderly themselves. This meant that most of the support given to Lilian was from people in Dave and Brenda's fellowship, of which the old lady was, as mentioned earlier, suspicious.

The lack of support from Michael, Lilian's son, was notable, but, surprisingly, seems to have caused Brenda little resentment.

There are still moments when Brenda feels pangs of guilt that her mum is no longer living with her, but she is convinced that the right decision was made. There is no bitterness or regret in Brenda's reminiscences of that stressful year spent caring for her mum. Instead, she looks back on the time as a period of growth and can see many ways in which God drew close to her.

References

1. Jurgen Moltmann, *The Crucified God*, SCM, 1974.
2. Joni Eareckson Tada, *Glorious Intruder; God's Presence in Life's Chaos*, Scripture Press, 1989.
Lord Longford, *Suffering and Hope*, Harper Collins, 1990.
3. Contact Revd Michael Wright, 25 Thornfield Road, Middlesbrough, Cleveland, TS5 5DD, sending an A4 stamped addressed envelope.
4. Contact Church Action on Disability (CHAD), Charisma Cottage, Drewsteignton, Exeter EX6 6QR.
5. Elisabeth Davies-Johns, *It's More Than Installing a Ramp; Ministry Alongside Those With Disabilities*, Methodist Publishing House, 1990.
6. Martyn Eden, David Potter and Terry Thompson, *No Handicaps Please, We're Christians; The Challenge of Disability*, Causeway (PO Box 351, Reading RG1 7AL), 1990.
7. National Retreat Association, National Retreat Centre, Liddon House, 24 South Audley Street, London W1Y 5DL, 071 493 3534.

4. If only they understood

The 5th October 1973 was a traumatic day for Carol. It was exactly a year since her first-born, a multiply-handicapped premature baby boy, had died at a few days old. She found herself back in the maternity hospital. Several weeks overdue, she had been in labour for three days and was only half conscious, as a result of the drugs she had been given.

Had Carol been fully alert, she would never have allowed doctors to make the mistake that was to affect her for the rest of her life. Failing to read her medical notes, doctors were unaware that Carol was allergic to anaesthetic. The dose they administered provoked a violent reaction in Carol. The cardiac arrest she suffered almost resulted in the death of the child she was carrying. It was a full forty-five minutes before the baby girl took her first breath.

When Carol regained consciousness, she discovered that her daughter had been taken to another hospital. She soon began to suspect that the consultant was ignoring her. Becoming anxious and bewildered, she demanded a conversation with the consultant. She told the doctor she would like to see the child, but remembers being told that, since the child would die anyway, there was no point in Carol seeing her.

Carol was puzzled when, shortly afterwards, she was moved across

75

the hospital to a ward of her own. The staff nurse confessed that she was under orders not to allow Carol to mix with the other patients. The kindly nurse disregarded her orders and allowed Carol to mix with those close to her ward. After 10 days of agonising waiting, Carol was reunited with her baby, the daughter she was to call Donna.

When Carol left hospital to return to her home and her husband, Martin, she had no idea what lay ahead. While Donna had been severely damaged at birth, there was no telling what would be the extent of her permanent disability. In some ways, looking after Donna was much the same as caring for any child, though. All babies are helpless, thought Carol. The major difference in those early days was that Donna could not establish a pattern of sleep and, as a consequence, screamed constantly and allowed Carol very little sleep.

Carol admits that, in the immediate aftermath of Donna's birth, she did not face up to her feelings. After her first child died she had put behind her the sadness and fear, and decided to have another child immediately. Now, faced with a second tragedy, the young mum was so caught up in the practical demands of caring for her child that she had little time or energy for coming to terms with her own sense of loss. Her mother, a nurse, had never allowed her to express sadness, and it was to this 'stiff upper lip' mentality that Carol resorted.

Carol also feared that, should she admit she was not coping, her child would be removed and taken into care. When her health visitor and GP asked how she was, she would tell them she was fine. Inside her, however, raged a storm. She found that it was difficult to love this child who had brought so much pain. She was bitter towards God for dealing her a second blow. She stopped going to church.

It was the kind words of a former vicar which enabled Carol to come to terms with her life. He told her that she had special qualities so that God had entrusted her with a child who needed a great deal of love and care. From then on, Carol felt she could love and accept Donna. Her bitterness ended, and she began once more to go to church.

As Donna developed, the extent of her disabilities became apparent. It was evident that, in physical terms, Donna's was a severe case of cerebral palsy. She never learned to walk and her co-ordination was so poor that she could do little for herself. But Carol felt she had reason to feel encouraged. Mentally, the little girl was obviously very bright. Miraculously, and defying probability, the 45 minute ordeal at birth, prior to taking her first breath, had not left Donna with a mental disability.

Donna could scarcely speak, but there was one desire which she communicated to her mother in no uncertain terms. She was lonely and there was nothing she would like more than a younger brother or sister. Carol felt for her child. Many were the times when, on occasions when the little girl was left in her pushchair on the grass the family shared with other families on their council estate, other mothers would rush to take their children back home. None of the parents were brave enough to encourage their offspring to involve Donna in their games.

It was, therefore, mainly for Donna's sake that Carol and Martin decided to have another child. But it was also for Carol's sake; she needed to prove to herself that she was capable of bearing a healthy child. Doctors were not prepared to take any risks. In the early stages of Carol's pregnancy they decided she would need weekly check-ups, that the birth would be induced before distress signals appeared, and that it would be by Caesarean section.

Determined that Donna would feel a part of the experience, Carol took her six-year-old daughter to every hospital appointment related to the pregnancy. She asked the staff at the hospital if it would be possible for Donna to see the baby before anyone else. Her wish was fulfilled and Donna was able to announce proudly that she alone had seen Andrew, the little boy who peacefully and uneventfully joined the family that momentous day. Not only were Donna's dreams realised, Carol had demonstrated that she was capable of giving birth to an able-bodied baby.

Carol never once regretted taking the fearful step of carrying a third child. Caring for two dependent children was not easy, but the joy Andrew brought to the family more than compensated for the extra work. Donna showed not an ounce of jealousy. Carol's midwife, a friend from church, enthusiastically included Donna in her care of the baby. Carol recalls fondly the happy times of quiet while, breast-feeding Andrew, she would read stories to Donna. As the baby grew into a little boy, he returned his sister's affection. The two adored each other.

All was not well in the family, however. Perhaps it was observing the development of his healthy child that made Martin realise the extent of the demands Donna's disability placed upon the family. He began to resent the time and energy Carol needed to devote to caring for Donna. There were few opportunities for him to spend time alone with his wife. He thought how much more pleasant life would be were it shared only with Carol and Andrew. He turned to alcohol as a refuge and this, in turn, caused him to be violent towards his wife.

Eventually, he gave Carol an ultimatum. If she did not put Donna in a home and forget about her, concentrating her affections on her marriage and son, he would leave. Carol was faced with a decision no one should have to make. She must choose between her husband and her child. But she never doubted what her conclusion would be. Donna had not asked to live a life of pain and disability. She deserved to be loved, not abandoned.

Martin left. He moved in with another woman and they now have two children. Donna was relieved. She had witnessed the fights, the beatings to which her mother had been subject. She was glad that tranquility had been restored to the household. Carol too felt initial relief and was too busy looking after her children to examine her feelings closely. It was Andrew who, at five years of age, suffered the most when Martin walked out on the family. Andrew is now 11, he sees Martin twice a week, but he still cannot understand why he no longer lives with his dad. So great was the hurt Andrew sustained that he continues to have difficulty learning and is receiving counselling at school. Carol feels helpless to comfort him in his grief.

Carol feels no bitterness towards Martin. She accepts that he does not have within him the resources to live with and care intimately for a disabled child. She does admit, though, that life as a single parent has been much harder. In the six years since her marriage broke up she has felt the loss of someone to whom to turn in a crisis. She struggles to be mother and father to her children.

In many ways, Carol feels she has been inadequate as a parent. She blames herself for Donna's disability. An insensitive doctor, following Donna's birth, had told her that if she had not been stupid enough to react to the anaesthetic, her child would not have been harmed. She still lives with the guilt which this remark induced.

She also feels she has not offered Andrew what he has needed. A couple of years ago Andrew asked Carol why she spent so much time looking after Donna, and none with him. She realised how neglected he must feel. Andrew had shown an interest in learning to play the piano and flute. She resolved to find lessons for him and now spends time each day helping him with his music. She is so pleased that he is excelling in it and that she has found a way to give him her time and attention.

Donna has left school and is now enjoying a course in a local college. She hopes to live at home for the foreseeable future and to this end the family's council-owned bungalow has been adapted to help her to be as independent as possible. Carol firmly believes Donna has the right to decide where she lives. She is pleased that Donna has chosen to stay at home and confesses that she would find life hard if Donna moved out. Should anything happen to Carol, the two have decided that Donna will, if possible, receive the help she needs to remain living in the bungalow. Carol in no way expects Andrew to care for his sister in the future; she even fears that caring at close quarters may spoil the close relationship the two now enjoy.

Following her divorce, Carol cannot seek paid work. Were she to be in paid employment, she would lose custody of Donna. Instead, she spends the time when Donna and Andrew are out during the day helping other carers in a voluntary capacity. She lives on Income Support and disability allowances which barely cover the extra costs she incurs through looking after a disabled child. She never has a holiday, and the few services she has received (such as help with laundry) are gradually being cut back.

It has only been in the last year that Carol has faced up to her grief and loneliness. Through talking to other carers, she has come to acknowledge the pain associated with caring for a disabled child. As the children grow older, she does not look forward to the future, knowing if Donna left she would be on her own. Donna has ongoing health problems. She has been frequently hospitalised, coming dangerously close to death three years ago when she was struck down with encephalitis which rendered her even more disabled, incontinent and unable to hold herself up. Presently, she has frequent, alarming convulsions (sometimes five or six a day) and problems with the tube leading to her stomach which requires an operation. Her speech is incomprehensible to those outside the family, so she has recently been given a 'touch talker'. Carol is hoping to acquire a home computer for her in the near future which would further aid her communication.

Carol's life is undeniably difficult, but she does not spend time thinking about her troubles. She loves and is proud of her children, Andrew's warmth and kindness, and Donna's courage and undying sense of humour. It is her mother love which fires the determination with which she strives for the best for each.

Problems relating

Caring for another person is essentially about a relationship. It is hardly surprising, then, that the difficulties which often cause carers the most anguish are difficulties in their relationships. The difficulties have a number of roots: they can spring from the fact that the carer is over-loaded with demands for nurturing; they can result from conflicts in the carer's relationships; and they can stem from the fact that the carer has no one to care for them.

The overloaded carer

When Donna, Carol's daughter with cerebral palsy, was a baby, the demands she placed upon her mother were similar to the demands any baby makes. As Donna grew, however, her dependency did not decrease. Indeed, encephalitis, which she contracted three years ago, rendered her yet more helpless. She needs help with all her bodily functions. She has even to be turned in bed several times each night. At 17, her weight is that of an adult, so that lifting her is no simple task. In addition, she now suffers regular convulsions, calling for constant vigilance on Carol's part.

You might say that Carol has her hands full! As well as the obvious physical demands upon her time which come with caring for her disabled daughter, however, there are more subtle pressures on Carol. The carefully tuned sensitivity between a parent and their helpless baby never died in Carol's relationship with Donna. She is at all times ready to respond to her child's needs, listening always, constantly alert. Donna can never be far away from her thoughts. Donna's health has always given cause for concern, so that Carol cannot help but spend some of her time worrying about it, constantly monitoring the effects of the many drugs she takes to keep her condition under control. Is it any wonder that Andrew felt his mother's time and energy was not directed at meeting his needs?

The sad fact of the matter is that so many carers feel that they have let down one or other of their relatives through channelling so much attention into looking after the disabled person. This awareness is particularly acute where the carer's other children are concerned. In a sense it makes little difference for whom they are caring – a disabled child, a sick spouse, or a frail elderly person – there persists a sense that the carer's children are missing out. The carer knows they are less available for leisurely conversation, for heart to heart discussions about their children's growing-up problems, than are other parents. They feel acutely the recognition that their children are missing out on the pleasures other families share: family outings; summer holidays; sport and other recreational activities.

To sustain a deep, mutually beneficial relationship with one's children as a carer can be difficult. To nurture a loving, supportive marriage can be just as, if not more, problematic. It is not unknown for a marriage to flounder when children arrive. The helpless new baby, diverting the energies of perhaps one partner in particular, can provoke resentment in the other. The couple perhaps become vulnerable to sexual problems. In a family where one member cares for another who is disabled, the same dynamics can be at work in a marriage. Imagine the sense of conflicting loyalties for carers of elderly parents. In-law relationships can be fraught at the best of times. With the added stress of disability they can become very tense. The carer then feels pulled between their spouse and their parent. Marriages require careful nurturing. They need considerable time if they are to flourish.

Carol and Martin's marriage was not given the space and time which it needed. The reasons behind this were complex. Carol was afraid Donna would be taken away from her, so that she was reluctant to admit she needed help. At the risk of making a political statement, I would conjecture that, had she been forthright in asking for help, it may not have been given in the quantity or shape most conducive to enhancing married life. Carol now assents to the suggestion that, had she and Martin spent more time together alone, their marriage may have been intact to this day. Because their relationship was squeezed too hard by the demands of caring, its survival was threatened. Sadly, the divorce rate among parents of disabled children is alarmingly high.

Undoubtedly the greatest demands placed upon the carer are from people living in the same household, but, to understand the range of pressures they face, we must look further afield. Each carer will have relatives and friends beyond their immediate household who appear to have a legitimate claim upon their energies. Extended family members – a parent, a grown-up child, an aunt, a grandfather – may comment that they would like to see the carer more often. Other friends and relatives are more discreet, but the carer feels aggrieved that they are unable to devote quality time to relationships with them. Picture a scenario where the mother of a disabled child is pained by the awareness that her widowed father is lonely and sad and living some twenty or thirty miles away, but feels powerless to help.

Living with the tension of conflicting demands within relationships which are legitimate and important to the carer can be intolerable. To close, however, we must remark upon a final set of demands which are not, in my opinion, valid. These demands are the consequence of the *persona* which a carer can easily acquire. It goes without saying that carers are caring people. The impetus to protect and nurture someone who is vulnerable is well developed in them, either by choice or necessity. There is a danger that needy folk will be drawn to them. In chapter 3 we saw how Brenda was called upon to help, not only by her disabled mother, but by many people in need in her church fellowship. It was a ministry she enjoyed, but it meant that not only was she coping with demands from her disabled mother, her husband and her two children, but she was also taking upon herself a multitude of problems originating from outside her own family.

The carer in conflict

It is not difficult to envisage how these tensions in the relationships of carers spill over into situations of conflict and confrontation. Every one of us needs time for self. When the demands of those around us deprive us of opportunity for self-regeneration, it is likely that our dealings with them will become irritable.

The relationship most vulnerable to conflict is the carer's relationship with the person for whom they care. It is important to preface this discussion with the realisation that it is usually a relationship of great reward. Carol's relationship with daughter Donna, as we saw earlier, is one of affection and mutual respect and trust. While believing Donna must make her own decisions regarding her future, it is Carol's cherished hope that she will decide to continue living at home, because she enjoys her daughter's company. Keith and Janet's relationship, in the introductory chapter, epitomises a marriage where one spouse's limitations in no way undermine the bond of mutual and equal love and affection.

Having said this, the relationship between a disabled person and their carer can be troublesome. Problems can be provoked by any number of factors. Much will depend upon the relationship between the two. Adults caring for their elderly parents can find the dynamics of the situation especially trying. There may have developed an emotional distance, not to mention a geographical separation, between the adult child and their parent. The relationship may have had a history of conflict and tension which is not easily overcome when caring flings the two into enforced intimacy. Furthermore, to be looking after one's parents is a reversal of roles which can seem unnatural and strange.

Other relationships may have their delicate balance upset by caring, but in a different way. The carer might find themself performing intimate personal care tasks for their husband or wife, something which can interfere with the dynamics of their sex life. Many illnesses and disabilities themselves restrict opportunities for relating in a sexual way.

The potential for conflict is not only dependent on the relationship between the carer and the disabled person. It is affected too by the stage along the caring process which the two have reached. The early days of caring are possibly those most vulnerable to tensions. Not only must the disabled person come to terms with devastating loss (of health, of employment, of physical ability), but the carer must adjust to the changes in their relationship with the disabled person and to the new demands placed upon them.

Having noted the factors which influence conflict (the relationship between the disabled person and the carer, and the stage along the caring process at which the two have arrived), we can now look at the sources of conflict which can arise. Often the irritability manifested by both carer and cared-for person is simply a response of anger to a seemingly hopeless and intractable problem. How easy it is to vent pent-up feelings of misery and frustration on the ones we love. We shall see later in the chapter that Gillian's mentally handicapped son, Robert, releases his anger in the presence of his principal carer, his mum.

Some disagreements are the consequence of clashes of temperament. Blood ties do not equate with harmonising personalities, as many a carer looking after a frail parent will testify. It may be possible to live with the things in your parent, or child, which irritate you, if you see them a few times each year. But living under the same roof can bring tensions to the surface and manufacture explosive situations.

Another source of conflict can be the personality changes which illness can bring about. Some illnesses, or the drugs used to treat them, effect radical change in the sufferer. For others, the mere fact of disability and dependency can bring about a self-pitying frame of mind in a hitherto positive, cheerful character. The sweet old lady becomes a hectoring tyrant. The carers of victims of mental illnesses deserve special mention at this point. Such conditions radically alter the mindset of the sufferer and can induce very hurtful responses to the carer. The schizophrenia sufferer may be subject to paranoid delusions, convinced even that close relatives are plotting against them. The Alzheimer's patient, too, is prone to paranoia, and in the later stages of the illness may not even recognise their loved ones. Many carers of depression sufferers endure the pain of rejection when their attempts to console and offer comfort are spurned. Many such illnesses rob carers of a fulfilling, loving relationship suddenly and without warning. They can find that the person to whom they are relating is someone entirely unfamiliar.

Finally, some of the conflicts are simply over differences of opinion or preference. Some sick people, particularly those with mental illnesses, disagree with their carers that they have a problem at all. The initial dispute is over whether or not to seek medical help. Conflicts can also arise over the balance of care which the disabled person should receive. The carer may feel that day care would be beneficial, while their relative would rather be at home during the day. The disabled person may wish to live as independent a life as possible, in their own home, while the carer feels more secure with their relative under the same roof. Ironically, the carer's attempts at securing respite may be thwarted by the disabled person's reluctance to be taken out of the safe and familiar surroundings of the family home.

It would be wrong to give the impression, however, that the conflicts surrounding caring reside exclusively in the relationship between the disabled person and their carer. Gillian's story, which will be recounted later on in the chapter, illustrates well the tensions which can exist between parents of disabled children. Differences of approach can set spouses at emnity with one another. In 'Mummy, Why Have I Got Down's Syndrome?', Caroline Philps describes the conflict she and her husband experienced over their differing methods of helping their daughter Elizabeth Joy.(1) Caroline was inclined to work very hard at helping Elizabeth to acquire skills, while her husband's approach was more relaxed. In Martin and Carol's case, differences of opinion over Donna proved irreconcilable and their marriage ended. When Carol refused to find permanent residential care for Donna, Martin's behaviour became increasingly aggressive before he eventually left the family.

In-law relationships can cause problems for carers, as we mentioned earlier. Imagine how easy it is to resent a mother- or father-in-law who moves into your home and seems to dominate your spouse's time and energy. Conflict can easily result.

Finally, conflict can occur between family carers and formal carers of the disabled person. The parents of a child with learning difficulties may feel strongly, against the judgment of professionals working with the family, that their daughter or son should be integrated within the mainstream education system. This conflict over education arose for Gillian and her family, as we will see later. In many and varied ways, carers can feel that their opinions are undermined or ignored by doctors or social workers.

The gravity of tensions within the caring relationship should never be overlooked. They can place a vulnerable sick person at severe risk. This was highlighted by a recent survey by Crossroads in which 13 per cent of carers said they often felt like being violent towards their relative.(2) This temptation to be violent is something which shames and alarms carers. The caring relationship should never be allowed to deteriorate to the point at which such extremes are the final resort of an individual who is at breaking point.

The isolated carer

The isolation which so many carers experience is often more about a state of mind than a set of circumstances. In certain ways carers can feel that everyone around them fails to perceive or understand their predicament. We look first, however, at the circumstances which can contribute to a carer becoming cut off from the world.

Many carers find that the demands of their role lead to them being denied the structured settings through which most of us meet other people. The most significant of these settings is the workplace. Many carers do struggle to remain in employment, but a good deal more find that it becomes an intolerable strain. Of those surveyed by Crossroads recently, half of the carers had been forced to give up work to care for their disabled relative or friend.(3) Perhaps the carer finds that their concentration at work is lapsing because they are worrying about how their relative is faring at home. Maybe they are constantly exhausted, finding that instead of being able to relax after a hard day at the office, they must begin again on their equally tiring second job, that of caring. Finally, it may be the case that they are called upon to spend an ever-growing number of days at home whilst their relative's health goes through a crisis. Unfortunately, contracts of employment do not always offer the flexibility which would be ideal for carers.

For whatever reason, and however willingly, the carer may resign from work and suddenly find themself confined to the home for the best part of the week. They no longer have the daily stimulus of conversation with colleagues. For the parent of a disabled child, the break with work may come slightly differently. Instead of being able to return to work several months, or years, after the child's birth, they find themselves compelled to remain at home indefinitely.

There are other ways in which carers lose opportunities to mix with other people. When a skilled sitter, even a nurse, must be found for each occasion when the carer wishes to spend an evening out, the inclination is to stay at home. Even in cases where the carer is prepared to pay, sitting services do not come cheap.

Just as meeting new people can be extremely difficult, sustaining old friendships can present problems. A carer's friend may feel that they are having to take all the initiative in sustaining their relationship with the carer. Their enthusiasm for doing so may wane if they interpret the carer's reticence as a polite rebuff. The friend may also have difficulty overcoming their own fear of visiting the home of an invalid, of talking to the carer about what appears to be a very traumatic situation. At the moment when the friend is most needed, they distance themself from the carer who in turn feels rejected and lonely.

The social isolation to which carers are prone is perhaps most severe for unmarried people. Many married carers express sympathy for their counterparts who lack the support of a caring partner. There is a sense, however, in which even when a carer is surrounded by other people, they feel cut off from those around them. They feel those with whom they share their lives have neither the willingness nor the capacity to enter into the experience they face. They may feel their disabled relative is so absorbed in their own pain that they are unable to identify with their carer's feelings. Other family members may themselves be hurting and also lack the wherewithal to look outward. Thoughtless remarks from those outside the family reveal the lack of comprehension of the carer's plight.

Many carers feel that no one is there for them. Those around them assume they are somehow fulfilled and self-contained in their caring role. No one, it feels, thinks to ask how they are feeling. Statistics can mislead, but when two-thirds of carers recently interviewed said that no one ever listened to them, it seems to sum up what carers feel about this isolation.(4)

Helping carers

Helping the over-loaded carer

Family relationships are the most delicate of things. Concerned outsiders can wreak havoc by attempting to remedy a problem which they perceive to have arisen within them. In helping a carer to feel they have space and time to develop each of the relationships important to them, sensitivity is needed. Unless the carer makes clear that they would rather not discuss their intimate relationships, we could perhaps seek opportunities to talk through which, if any, of their relationships, they feel needs extra time and how to help.

Both families in this chapter demonstrate the importance of allowing time for the carer's marriage to be nurtured. There is no other way for this to happen than for a couple to be given time together alone. The solution is found in another person taking over from the carer for a few hours, even a few days, from time to time. Caring friends who volunteer to sit with the disabled person are much appreciated. It helps if this type of support is regular and reliable. You may feel unequal to the task of caring for a disabled person. Talk through with the carer what is involved to assess whether or not you are capable of helping. If you feel unequal to the task, perhaps you can identify another friend who would be better suited to it.

Such 'respite' care, as it is known, can prove beneficial, not only to the carer's marriage, but to their relationships with other relatives. It can allow time for the carer to be with their able-bodied children, or with members of the wider family. In some senses, however, the carer cannot be everything they would like to be to each of the relatives placing demands upon them. They have only limited time and energy to invest. When this is the case, our role as a friend of the carer, is two-fold.

We must first allow our carer friend to acknowledge and come to terms with the fact that their human resources are circumscribed. They may lack the time and energy to be the perfect parent to each of their children, the ideal wife or husband for their spouse. But there are no perfect parents or partners. Each of us fails our relatives somewhere along the line. The carer must be steered away from demoralising self-recrimination and helped to see that they are doing the best they can.

Secondly, perhaps there are ways in which we can supplement what the carer is able to give to each of their relatives. Perhaps the younger brother or sister of a mentally handicapped child is losing out in some ways as a result of their sibling's disability. It may be appropriate for a friend of the family to take on that child as a special concern, praying for the child, taking them out for the day from time to time, building up a trusting friendship. There might be a member of the wider family who is missing out on the practical help or social visits they would need. A friend of the family might well be able to offer friendship or help around the house that would go some way towards making up for the time the carer is unable to give.

A friend of a carer can, thus, help them to fulfil some of their responsibilities, while sharing others. Finally, a friend can also help shield the carer from unnecessary burdens, the problems off-loaded onto them because of their caring *persona*. The friend can ensure, for instance, that unthinking members of churches do not make the assumption that, because the carer spends much time at home, they have limitless time to befriend and counsel those in need in the church. Of course, the carer may indeed wish to do this, but a caring friend can make sure that their inclination to extend yet further their caring resources is not taken for granted.

Helping the carer through conflict

Diplomacy in the utmost is needed in helping a carer resolve tensions which arise in their family. With care, a constructive role can be found by the carer's Christian friends. There are two facets to this role. The first facet is more passive than the other, and concerns approach. The second, active facet is about taking positive steps to help resolve and to minimise conflict.

As Christians we should be experts in helping individuals resolve tensions in their relationships! Our faith is all about reconciliation. Our God reconciled us to himself through the death of his Son. Through him we can find inner peace, and peace with those around us. Unfortunately, our other nature often gets the better of us and we take pleasure in confrontation. Our obstacle in helping carers resolve conflict with loved ones is that, while expressing concern, we need to help defuse tension. In adopting a helpful approach, it is important that we do not take sides. We need to remember, when talking with the carer about disagreements with the person for whom they care, for example, that we hear only their side of the argument. We need to avoid casting their relative in the role of guilty party.

At the same time as avoiding taking sides ourselves, we need to help the carer to see the situation from the perspective of the relative with whom they are in conflict. In response to their statements about the issue in question, we could perhaps ask, 'How do you think Martin sees it?' or, 'Why do you think Jane is reacting in that way?' etc.

Moving on to the positive steps we can take, having understood the root of the conflict between the carer and their friends or relatives, we can begin to take action which might help to resolve it.

It is most important in this process to avoid offering help which benefits the carer to the disadvantage of the disabled person, or *vice versa*. We need, in thinking creatively, to discover ways of contributing which have at heart the best interests of both. Offers of respite care need to be attractive to both the disabled person and their carer. They need to be solutions which nurture, socially and emotionally, and enhance the dignity of, the disabled person, while relieving the carer of the physical burden and anxiety involved in caring. We need to ask if the disabled person would prefer to spend time away from the carer in their own home, or in someone else's. Would they enjoy a change of scene, or would they feel more secure in their familiar home environment? In meeting the needs of the disabled person, through offering the carer respite, we minimise the risk of conflict between the two.

Helping the isolated carer

There are basically two ways, I feel, through which we can help relieve the sense of isolation into which many carers fall.

The first approach to helping is to look for ways in which to ensure that the carer's social networks do not dwindle. We mentioned earlier that carers often lose friendship through having to give up work. Many carers feel a tremendous sense of relief on making the decision, but others live with regret, hankering after that sphere of life where they confidently exercised skills, for which they were financially rewarded, and met and became close to a group of work-mates. Is there any way in which you could help a carer to remain in work? If you are an employer, it might be useful to become aware of those in your employ who are carers and to offer them greater flexibility in their working patterns. Alternatively, you might be a neighbour of a carer and able to pop in on the disabled person from time to time while the carer is at work, to check that they have everything they need.

There may be other activities which your carer friend is struggling to hold on to. They may be a member of a choir. Perhaps they enjoy attending a keep-fit class. There may be a sport which they like to play or watch. All these leisure activities have benefit in giving the carer interests outside the home and opportunity to socialise and make new friends. It is often difficult, however, for the carer to find someone to stand in for them for the couple of hours needed to pursue these hobbies, particularly in the evenings when most sitting services do not operate. Again, we come back to the idea of offering our services to sit with the disabled person. Instead, we might offer them hospitality in our home. Still there is the need, however, to ensure that we are capable of offering the care they would need.

Perhaps the most important of all the things we can do to

relieve the carer's sense of isolation, however, is to be faithful in our friendship. If we understand why it is that our carer friend is less able to initiate meetings with us, we will have the grace and humility, not to mention determination, to ensure that our friendship with them continues to be nurtured and provide a context in which our carer friend feels needed and valued. We need to continue our visits to the carer's home tenaciously. We can also ensure that we make a point of phoning regularly or, should we live some distance away, writing frequent letters.

In our friendship with the carer, the most valuable attribute we can bring is the ability to listen. Chapter 2 has given hints on developing listening skills and directs the reader to useful resources. You may feel, after a long conversation with the carer, that you have done little to help. But your affirmative nods, your undivided concentration on their troubles, your kind glances, will have gone a long way towards convincing them that there are people around them who care for them.

So many carers speak appreciatively of the constancy of their friends, whose faithful kindness offers an oasis from the stresses of their lives. Such friendship is a life-line for many, an anchor which prevents them from drifting hopelessly in the storm of life's troubles. Never underestimate the contribution you can make simply through 'being there' for the carer whenever you are needed.

Gillian feels that giving people labels can be destructive. It alters the way they are perceived and will often belittle them.

Gillian's son, Robert, was not given a label until he was four years of age. When he was two, and he seemed slow to speak, Gillian had taken him to the doctor. But a psychologist who examined Robert's progress said Gillian, and her husband Graham, were being too hard on the child. During the next two years the parents tried to ignore their doubts. They spent many a gruelling and frustrating hour attempting to teach Robert his colours and numbers. He seemed not to mind their insistence and eventually learned what they taught him. During that time, Emma, a second child, was born.

It was a handful of weeks before Robert was due to start at the local infant school when he was diagnosed as having mild learning difficulties. There is nothing in Robert's outward appearance to indicate his disability. It is only after speaking with him for a few minutes that those in conversation with him realise something is slightly amiss. This causes Gillian to feel that Robert's disability perhaps sprang from X-rays she was given in the early months of her pregnancy, following complications.

It was a shock for Gillian and Graham to have to adjust to the fact that their eldest child had special needs. They were shown around the local school for children who were ESN, but objected strongly to the thought that their son, whom they had treated for four years as normal, might be educated there. The school contained children with severe multiple handicaps. Requests for special tutoring within the local infant school were turned down. The suggestion that Robert travel some 15 miles to a more appropriate school, for children with mild learning difficulties, was dismissed as far too expensive.

Throughout Robert's schooling, therefore, he had severe behavioural difficulties, associated, in Gillian's mind, with the inappropriateness of his education. As he became taller and stronger, he expressed his frustration through fighting with other children. By the time he was 16 the staff were more than happy for him to leave. As planned, Robert left home for an agricultural college for those with learning difficulties. He spent two years there.

In many respects, Gillian feels that college did not work out for Robert. Graham and Gillian became distance carers, sometimes taking as many as six phone calls a day from their homesick son. Despite reports of his growing self-confidence from college staff, after two years at college Robert seemed to have lost many of the skills he possessed when he left home. Before college, Robert had had a Saturday job for a local farmer. He had quite happily shopped alone in town, using local bus services. When he returned from college, even walking down the road held terror for him.

Gillian realised she could not resume her old parental role in helping Robert overcome his fears, now he had turned 18. So the family employed a local girl for a few months to take Robert out while he regained confidence.

It was following Robert's return from college that tensions in the family surfaced. It became apparent that Graham and Gillian had fundamentally different approaches to Robert's needs. Gillian was inclined to see her son as an adult, capable of a measure of independence. She would have preferred him not to have returned home after college, but to live separately from the family, visiting them regularly. This philosophy led her to ask Robert to take care of many of his own domestic requirements, cleaning his own bedroom and washing and ironing his clothes.

Graham's attitude was protective. He felt he and his wife had a life-long responsibility directly to care for Robert. He favoured Robert living in the family home, and found Gillian's insistence that Robert take care of himself harsh. Another source of tension was Gillian's work. For several years, she had enjoyed a part-time job which held considerable responsibility. She felt that Graham's view was that she should be at home looking after Robert. He seemed to accuse her of selfishness.

Recognising that the family, and especially her marriage, needed help to survive, shortly after Robert's return Gillian began to pay to see a counsellor. She pays warm tribute to the help this has brought her. She says that, possibly for the first time in her life, she is learning to identify and assert what she wants out of life. She is recognising that she can determine her own future. For several months she in turn attempted to counsel Graham, but she found herself unable to sustain the emotional support he wanted. When she suggested he see a counsellor, she recalls, Graham became angry and refused.

Tensions were mounting. Robert resented his father's heavy-handed, autocratic interchanges with him and the two frequently shouted at one another. Robert was often unkind towards Emma, upsetting and angering her. Robert vented his frustrations upon Gillian, swearing and shouting at her. Gillian attempted to act as peacemaker, but her resources were minimal.

Marshalling the skills she had acquired through counselling, Gillian began to speak to the family about ways in which change needed to occur. She made clear to Emma that she should not tolerate Robert's unkindness; she should treat him in the way he treated her. She no longer kept up the pretence of concealing her own hurt feelings from Robert. When insulted by Robert, she began to cry openly, hoping that by so doing she would allow him to see the consequences of his actions. No longer would she intervene if family members quarrelled. She allowed them to settle their own differences.

Most important of all, Gillian set about attempting to ensure her marriage remained intact. Despite Graham's protestations, she insisted that she needed one weekend each month and one holiday a year alone with him. After two years of problems in finding the respite for Robert which this would demand, the two have taken their first holiday together for many years. Gillian has warned that, if suitable permanent accommodation for Robert outside the family home is not found within the next two years, she will leave Graham. She has told him she loves him and wants to spend her life with him, but is not prepared to spend her 40s and 50s caring for their son.

Gillian admits that she is not cut out to be a full-time carer. Only her work has kept her going over the years of looking after Robert. She is angry that, four years ago, when she told the authorities her family life was jeopardised by her caring responsibilities, nothing was done to help. It was left to her own initiative to arrange respite care. She is sad that expectations of Robert are so low. She feels that his ability to be adult and look after himself has been underestimated.

Gillian feels strongly that all carers should have access to a free counselling service. Only that way will their personal needs be recognised, affirmed and legitimised. Looking to the future, she does not anticipate her life will be dominated by caring. She prefers to think that her skills will be used in paid employment and in renewing the hobbies, such as painting, which she dropped when she started a family. After more than 20 years of being very caring, she says, she wants to spend the next 10 years meeting her own needs.

References

1. Caroline Philps, '*Mummy, Why Have I Got Down's Syndrome?*', Lion Publishing, 1991.
2. Crossroads Care, *Caring for Carers; a Nationwide Survey*, Association of Crossroads Care Attendant Schemes Ltd., 1990.
3. *ibid.*
4. *ibid.*

5. Not enough hours in a day

This book has deliberately focused in earlier chapters on the problems carers face in terms of feelings and relationships. The reasoning behind this emphasis has been two-fold. Firstly, it seems from my discussions with carers that these are the problems which cause them the greatest pain. Secondly, carers have also said to me that, while Christian friends have been willing to offer practical help, they have been reluctant to stand alongside them and be a listening ear through periods of emotional suffering.

It is nonetheless helpful if Christians are able to give practical support to their carer friends. This helps to reduce their tiredness and related vulnerability to lowness of mood. It also gives opportunity to establish a trust which may prompt the carer to confide their spiritual problems and relationship worries.

Some time ago I received a letter from Mr Anderson, who cares for his wife; she suffers from obstructive airways disease. He wanted to give me some impression of the stress he faced in caring for his wife. He wrote out a diary of his average day which illustrated remarkably well the practical demands so many carers face. I asked his permission to include the diary in this book.

A carer's average day

6.00 am Get up; make tea for patient; wash self; prepare antibiotic infusion for administering via a line direct into patient's subclavian vein (leading to the heart); set up equipment (patient connects herself to it); keep close watch to ensure correct drip rate, with no air bubbles

6.45 am Make tea and toast for self; eat/drink while preparing three packed lunches for teenage children; unload washing-machine; load dryer

7.15 am Disconnect infusion equipment; destroy non-reusable parts

7.30 am Call children (they get their own breakfast); help patient prepare inhalation therapy

8.00 am Unload dryer; fold ready for ironing (by home help)

8.15 am Make patient's bed and provide breakfast

8.30 am Go to work!

11.45 am Return home; help patient to get onto special bed (different room) and carry out physiotherapy procedures

12.15 pm Snack lunch for self and patient

12.30 pm Prepare antibiotic infusion etc (see 6.00 am procedure)

1.15 pm Go back to work . . .

5.30 pm Return home; cook prepared veg. (to go with auto-cooked meat etc)

6.15 pm Serve meal for patient, self and three children

6.45 pm Clear kitchen; prepare next day's meals

7.45 pm Visit local shop to buy next day's bread and any other essentials

8.15 pm Check patient; assist with preparing inhalation therapy and any other needs

8.30 pm Sort linen basket; load washing machine (for 'Economy 7' wash)

8.45 pm Check patient's surgical dressings; change as necessary (observing strict sterile procedures)

9.15 pm Rest on bed and wait for next antibiotic time

9.30 pm Prepare antibiotic infusion; set up equipment ready for patient to connect to self

10.00 pm Get into bed and stay awake until all treatments are finished; disconnect equipment; destroy non-reusable parts

11.30 pm   Settle down, hopefully until 6.30 am! Usually is a broken night

NB   The above is Monday–Friday schedule. Saturday to Sunday is similar except that time not spent at work is filled with: bathing patient; carrying out more physiotherapy treatment (I don't have time to provide the optimum needed on a weekday!); food shopping; house/garden/car maintenance; church (when treatment schedule permits).

A multiplicity of roles

It is clear, from reading Mr Anderson's diary, that the extreme pressures upon him are the result of the many different roles he fulfils. To enlarge upon this idea, we will look closely at each of those roles.

In the context of this book, it seems sensible to consider first Mr Anderson's role as carer. Many of the tasks he performs in helping his wife might be described as 'nursing tasks'. He prepares the medication she inhales and injects, and disposes of items required which are not re-usable. He administers physiotherapy. He changes her dressings. These jobs have to be done regularly, frequently and with unerring punctuality, if Mr Anderson's wife's condition is not to deteriorate.

Other carers have nursing tasks to undertake. They may not be administering drugs or physiotherapy, but they may be applying continence aids, or turning the patient regularly in bed to avoid pressure sores. If their relative is wheelchair-bound, they will certainly be involved in lifting them: from bed to wheelchair; from wheelchair to toilet; from car to wheelchair. They may do this many times each day, a strenuous element of caring, particularly for those caring for heavy adults.

These are some of the tasks we might expect a nurse to perform. Here is where the similarity with nursing ends, however. The first crucial difference between nursing and caring at home is that relatives rarely receive any training. This has two consequences. It means that tasks are more difficult and labour-intensive for carers. They take longer and are more taxing. It also means that they are prone to accidents. The second major dissimilarity is that carers often do their nursing in isolation. Whereas nurses are forbidden, for example, to lift a patient single-handed, carers, by force of circumstance, often do so on their own. This again leads to injuries such as back strain. Thirdly, carers are less fortunate than nurses in that to work a shift system is unknown to them. They cannot clock off after working contracted hours. They frequently continue caring, without breaks, until their own health disintegrates.

There are more subtle elements within the nursing role besides the obvious physical tasks many carers perform. In cases where the dependent relative is mobile, able to feed and toilet themself, they may still require supervision. A carer, for instance, cannot leave a mentally handicapped child. An Alzheimer's patient cannot be left alone in a room for very long. This represents a substantial restraint upon a carer's time.

This 'nursing' role, then, is undoubtedly the chief function fulfilled by carers. Many carers, like Mr Anderson, however, have a paid job too, either full-time or part-time. Mr Anderson explained, in his letter to me, that he very much regretted having to go out to work. He would much rather have spent more time at home with his wife. The financial circumstances of his family required that he earn a salary. In a later letter he explained that he had taken retirement two years early in order to give the increasing level of care his wife needed.

Attitudes to paid work amongst carers vary greatly. Brenda Baalham's husband, Chris, in *One in a Million*, was relieved when he decided to resign from work.(1) It meant that much of the help Brenda had been receiving from Christian friends, he was now able to take on himself. Clearly, before retiring, Mr Anderson too was overstretched, combining work and caring. In other cases, however, work is a lifeline for carers. It is the activity which maintains their links with the outside world, gives them an identity other than that of the extension of their disabled loved one, and helps them to sustain friendships. These carers would rather live with seemingly intolerable stress levels than give up a fulfilling area of their lives.

Through being a 'carer' and 'worker', many carers, then, are effectively doing two full-time jobs. On top of a 40 hour paid working week, they put in an additional 20, 30, even 40 hours a week, caring for their disabled relative. Instead of returning home in the evenings to rest, they resume tasks in the home which they left off in the morning, and often do not find time to sit down and relax until 10.00 pm or later. Their role is not dissimilar from that of a working parent of young children, only carers tend to be older and thus have less energy.

What other roles, besides 'carer' and 'worker', do carers assume? In Mr Anderson's case, it was being the second parent. His wife's illness meant that she was unable to contribute in a practical sense to the upbringing of their three children. He was doing jobs for which, perhaps, his wife had previously shared responsibility. In a slightly different way, we saw that Carol, in chapter 4, was both mother and father to her two children, as a result of her husband walking out on the family. The stresses of caring had driven her marriage apart, so that she now cared for her disabled daughter and able-bodied son, as a single-parent. She struggled in matching up to her dual parental role.

Many carers combine looking after a disabled relative, a parent for example, with raising young children. Some even have more than one sick or disabled person to care for. They struggle with competing pressures on their time.

For many carers, the task of 'home manager' too is either a new role, or one that becomes enlarged or more difficult. Many men who care have traditionally left household duties like cleaning and cooking to their wives. Even where such jobs have been evenly distributed, caring generates additional burdens. Suddenly the carer finds they are coping alone with running the home, perhaps grappling with some entirely unfamiliar tasks. In this respect, women can suffer too. Maybe they have left the payment of bills, or filling in forms, to their husband in the past. Now they are forced to do these things, because their husband is incapacitated.

Home management can, in any case, be more taxing in families involved in caring. For example, the disabled person may have difficulties with continence or with eating, so that their clothes require frequent washing. With disabilities such as cerebral palsy, clothes are subject to greater wear and tear, requiring frequent repairs. Some illnesses involve special diets, so that extra time must be spent by the carer in food preparation. In many ways, then, home management becomes more time-consuming.

It is clear from this description of some of the roles carers fulfil that their brief is indeed wide. Though receiving no training for the job, many see themselves as skilled in nursing, physiotherapy, cleaning, gardening, administration, cooking . . .

The distance factor

There are special pressures upon families in modern Britain. We make it especially difficult to fulfil this multiplicity of roles because we are such a mobile society. We are encouraged to uproot in the search for employment. We are not encouraged to consider the ramifications of this mobility for family life.

We shall see, later in the chapter, how Helen's difficulties in caring for her father were compounded by the distance separating their homes. Helen left her family home in the North East in her early 20s, to settle in London. At that stage a strategy for taking care of ailing, ageing parents was not something she considered.

Helen, like many carers, found that she was having to travel hundreds of miles each weekend to look after her disabled relative. Some carers are making a round trip of 50 miles each day to care for someone they love who lives in the next town. For someone who does not possess a car, this travelling can be especially taxing; even crossing a town to see a relative can involve several bus rides. There are further practical demands for carers who do not live in the same house as their disabled relative. They can easily find themselves in the position of having two homes to look after, two gardens to tend, two sittings each meal-time to prepare. Whichever house they are in, they are thinking about the many things which need doing in the other.

Not only does a mobile society leave many carers exhausted through constant travelling; it often means they are very isolated. It is simply not the case that extended families can easily share responsibility, for instance, for caring for a disabled parent. The load will probably fall unevenly on whichever son or daughter, son-in-law or daughter-in-law, lives nearest. We shall see later how difficult Helen and her brother and sister found it to divide caring for their father equally and harmoniously between themselves. While perhaps accepting that siblings live too far away to play a significant role in hands-on caring, many carers nevertheless feel exploited and resentful.

The money question

When Mr Anderson wrote to me, he mentioned that he was constantly overdrawn with the bank. He was unable to earn to the maximum of his capacity because of his caring duties. He was unable to give up work because he would not have managed financially. When he eventually decided, as he mentioned in a later letter, to retire early, he managed to cope financially only by taking a lump sum payment (which was quickly dwindling) and reducing his pension for the years to come.

Many experience a fall in family income as a result of caring. Disabled people themselves are amongst the poorest in our country and their carers suffer the same financial deprivation. Caring for a disabled person can be very expensive. They may require a special diet. If incontinent, there may be extra laundry costs. Certainly many carers find their heating bills soar. Then there is the special equipment, even house adaptations, that make disability more tolerable, but which can be expensive.

Put against these extra costs the reduced potential to earn a salary. Perhaps the mother of a child with cerebral palsy planned to return to work shortly after giving birth. It may prove impossible to find employment and so the family loses her income.

Unfortunately, financial benefits from the state go only a small way towards compensating for these costs and the loss of income-earning capacity. The result is that many carers live from month to month never knowing how they will pay the bills. In extreme cases, such as Pauline's in chapter 6, a carer may not even have enough money to feed herself adequately. The case studies in this book seem to bear out national statistics on the financial straits of single parents. Both single parents in this book living on state benefits have lived at subsistence level at some stage during their caring.

Services for carers

Before considering ways in which individual Christians can offer practical help to carers, we need to be aware of the support available to them from other sources. A number of sources might, in any one area, provide services aimed at helping carers. We shall look briefly at each.

First, we consider the benefits system. We referred, in the last section, on carers' financial affairs, to the benefits they can claim. Only two benefits are specifically geared towards helping carers: the Invalid Care Allowance (for people of working age) and the

Carer's Premium (for those on Income Support). Two other benefits, Mobility Allowance and Attendance Allowance, are targeted at disabled people, but are often used to contribute to the overall family income, thus indirectly benefiting carers. Retired carers, of course, receive the State Pension. Rules for claiming these benefits, governing ways in which they relate to each other, are complex. Often a carer is best advised to seek the services of a Welfare Rights Office or Citizens' Advice Bureau in claiming them.

A second source of services for carers is the local Social Services department. As things stand, many local authorities operate a home care service, or equivalent, meals-on-wheels, day centres, respite care in residential facilities, occupational therapy, aids and equipment, an incontinence laundry service and a voluntary family placement scheme. Some Social Services departments are appointing social workers, or other officers, to work specifically with carers.

A third, and perhaps equally important, source of help for carers is the local Health Authority. Some of the services carers can receive are hospital-based. Some carers are given respite care, with their relative spending say a fortnight a year in a hospital bed. Day hospitals give carers relief during the day. The Health Authority may also loan equipment. It may have residential facilities offering respite care. Very important, particularly for carers of terminally ill patients, are district nurses. Health visitors and community psychiatric nurses can also play a crucial role. Other services include chiropody, speech therapy, health promotion (including stress management courses), continence advice and physiotherapy.

The person who acts as gatekeeper for all these services, and whose role is fundamental in achieving adequate support structures for carers, is the GP. Unfortunately, the family doctor will often assume that carers are already aware of the financial benefits and practical help to which they are entitled. The GP is responsible for the carer's own state of health and can play a key role in recognising the point at which the carer is over-stretched and cannot carry on caring indefinitely.

The benefits system, Social Services department and Health Authority will be the chief statutory providers of help for any carer. Also impacting on their welfare, in many cases, are housing departments (giving council housing and home adaptations) and education authorities (providing special education, for instance).

There are, however, other agencies which have an important part to play in supporting carers. Many voluntary groups, including some church-based projects, have developed innovative schemes designed to relieve the stresses carers feel. The largest of these is Crossroads Care. Most major towns and cities now have Crossroads Care Attendant Schemes. Each scheme operates independently. Its funding base will be unique, but frequently grants are received from local authorities and health authorities. Care attendants give each family several hours each week when they go into the home and undertake those tasks which the carer would otherwise be doing, whilst the carer herself has a break.

Other voluntary sector schemes for carers include sitting services, telephone help and information lines and carers support groups (self-help organisations in which carers offer each other support and friendship). Finally, carers who can afford to may purchase help from commercial companies. Many aids for disabled people are produced by commercial organisations. Similarly, an increasing number of companies provide help within the homes of disabled people for a fee. Also private residential homes can sometimes hold short-term beds, allowing carers to take a two-week break, for instance.

From the point of view of carers, these services offer several main functions. Some are evidently designed to offer financial recompense to carers. Others give carers a break, either for a few hours each week, or for longer periods of several weeks. Others provide practical help within the carer's home. The prime goal of a small group of services is to give advice, information and emotional support for carers.

The above list looks, at first sight, like an impressive array of services, all targeted at helping carers. For several reasons, many carers feel the help that is available to them is inadequate, however. Many of the services have, as their main focus, the disabled person the carer looks after. This means that, when they do relieve the carer's burden, they only do so indirectly. It also means that, where resources are limited, the strains placed upon carers will not be the prime consideration in allocating them. The home help services, for example, will be targeted primarily at helping elderly people living on their own, rather than those living with relatives.

Another factor influencing the availability of services for carers is as basic as geography. There are frustrating regional variations in the help provided by Social Services, with some areas being particularly disadvantaged. Some local authorities have an explicit policy of supporting carers, whilst others do not. In some towns, attempts to set up Crossroads schemes have been thwarted by lack of funding. It can be frustrating for a carer who moves house to find that the services they found useful in their old town are not available in the area in which they have been relocated.

A related problem with the services available is the difficulty in finding out about them. Because help is available from such a disparate array of agencies, getting to know where it is and what it entails can prove daunting. The government has recognised this, and the National Health Service and Community Care Act of 1990 is an attempt to remedy the problem. The full effect of the legislation upon carers is yet to be seen, following delays in its implementation. Uncertainty regarding funding, in particular, means that the nature and extent of changes likely to occur from the spring of 1993 onwards are unknown. The basic goal of the Act and its provisions is to simplify community care, by giving overall responsibility for it to Social Services departments within local authorities. Where a person requires support in the community, they will be appointed a 'case manager', who will probably be a social worker. The case manager will hold a budget with which to buy in the services required, based on an assessment of need which they have made. In practical terms, this is intended to increase options. For example, instead of automatically finding themselves in a residential home when frailty strikes, elderly people will have greater opportunity to receive care in their own homes. To help Social Services departments to pay for this help, they will be given control over the funds from the social security budget hitherto used to pay fees for residential homes.

For up-to-date information about the implementation of the Act, and ways in which it effects carers you know, you would be advised to contact your local Social Services department. Be aware that we live in times of change where community care is concerned and that provision of services to support carers is set to change radically over the coming years. For the time being, some badly needed services are undersubscribed because carers remain ignorant of their existence.

Some carers do not claim benefits and services to which they are entitled because they simply do not realise that they can receive help in fulfilling what they perceive to be a personal responsibility. Perhaps they do not feel they need or deserve support. Maybe they feel that accepting it would be an act of disloyalty towards their disabled relative.

On the other hand, carers who do claim benefits and receive services are dissatisfied with them. The benefits, they feel, do not go far enough in acknowledging the financial sacrifices they make through caring. Services are not given in the manner, or during the times of day, which they would prefer. Sometimes help is only available during the working day, for instance, whilst the carer is at their most stressed first thing in the morning, or last thing at night. Often services lack reliability, with paid workers not visiting at the time promised, for instance. Many carers feel the care given is inferior to the care they can provide and are not willing to subject their relative to substandard support.

For all these reasons, and despite the commitment and professionalism of so many dedicated workers employed by the state or independent companies, only a tiny minority of carers receive any paid help at all in their caring. The people from whom they are most likely to be receiving help are their friends and relatives.

Lightening the load

If we are to help relieve some of the practical demands placed upon carers, we must remember three things in particular. We need to recognise our limitations. There are practical tasks in which we are not skilled. Unless we have training, administering injections, for instance, is something we must avoid. The second point to bear in mind is that we should consult our carer friend to establish with which tasks they would most appreciate help. Thirdly, some carers have said to me that, whilst general offers of help are very kind, they can be a little maddening! They would prefer to know exactly the nature and frequency of help we are able to give. In short, the message is that we must be specific.

Remembering these three points, we can now look at practical ways in which we can relieve the stress faced by carers. The first set of suggestions are aimed at releasing the carer's time and energy for their primary concern, caring for their disabled relative. The second group of ideas are for helping with the caring itself. The final recommendations are for enabling carers to receive the vital information which would enable them to access the practical help on offer from statutory, voluntary and commercial organisations.

We saw earlier in the chapter that carers have a great number of roles to play: carer; worker; second parent; home keeper; gardener. Their time is at a premium. If choices must be made between household tasks and caring, the majority will choose the latter. With a bit of sensitivity and insight, we can perhaps identify those responsibilities which detract the carer's energies from caring. If there are tasks to which the carer is unused (because their spouse formerly had responsibility for them, for instance), we could perhaps share them with the carer. Perhaps there are some jobs which the carer does not enjoy. We could offer to help with them. These jobs might include gardening, washing, ironing, housework, or car maintenance.

Often just a little extra thought and effort on our part can make a big difference to a carer's day. For example, we might pop in on a carer on the way to the shops, and offer to fetch groceries or a prescription. We could bake a few extra cakes or biscuits and take them to the carer's home. The carer might even be happy for us to cook a meal for their family in their own kitchen. Consummate tact and sensitivity are needed. Otherwise our gestures could be received as intrusive, or an implicit criticism of the carer's ability to cope. All these simple forms of help release a carer to take a rest or to spend time caring.

Depending on our own experience or training, there may be ways in which we can help the carer with the caring itself. We noted earlier how, though many of their tasks resembled those performed by nurses, carers are constantly on duty. Someone with nursing skills, perhaps, or with personal experience of caring for a sick or disabled relative, could step in and relieve the carer on an *ad hoc*, or regular, basis. They could be on hand to take the disabled person to the toilet, or to turn them in bed during the night. Even helping to push a wheelchair is much appreciated, particularly by carers who are themselves elderly or disabled. We need, in helping carers in their caring, to be aware of the needs of the disabled person. We must not run the risk of embarrassing them in the tasks we offer to do.

A final area of practical support we can offer is in helping carers to find out about the services and benefits which they are able to claim. This sounds simple, but can be quite complex, requiring several phone calls and visits to relevant offices to explore possibilities. More indirectly, your role could be to encourage the carer to take their own action, perhaps suggesting they contact the local Social Services department or Benefits office. Helping the carer to realise they both need and deserve help is crucial in overcoming the barriers some carers erect which impede them from reaching out for support. In more formal terms, this activity, in pushing for services for disabled people and their caring relatives, is known as 'advocacy'. Social Services departments have begun to turn to local church folk to act as advocates for, for instance, frail elderly people in residential homes. Perhaps you could be an 'advocate', formally or informally, for a family you know.

Some useful guides have been produced to help carers find out about the support available to them. If you could purchase for a carer with whom you are friendly the guide *Caring at Home*, or a more recent handbook, *Help at Hand*, you should find that they prove very useful.(2) Other guides, such as *The A–Z of Disability*, give more general information on where to find help in coping with disability.(3) All three guides contain much of the information on services, benefits and support of which carers can make use.

There is no short cut to offering relevant, welcome practical help to carers. Such help must be underpinned by friendship. Only when we know a carer well will we know when and how to offer them the help they so very much need.

Helen is a carer who faces the stresses of constant travelling in her efforts to care for her elderly father.

Though she is now 49, Helen's accent still contains traces of her Northumbrian childhood. She was raised the middle child of a strict Plymouth Brethren family hailing from rural Northumbria. In two crucial respects, however, Helen turned her back on those roots. While she was a teenager, she had wholeheartedly accepted, even promulgated, her parents' faith, but when adulthood arrived Helen began to have doubts about their creed. By the age of 22, she had rejected it altogether. Life at home became difficult, as her parents adjusted to Helen's decision, so that she soon felt it was necessary to take a second big step away from her upbringing. In order to become her own independent person she, as her brother was also later to do, followed her sister down to London, and established a home in her heart for the capital.

A talented young woman, Helen soon rose to a senior rank in the Civil Service, working for the Treasury. It was not until she reached her early 40s that she began questioning some of the values that underpinned that institution. She hit a personal crisis, during which she investigated many of the world's major belief systems, searching for some answer to her moral dilemmas. In Eastern mysticism she found ideas that made sense in her situation, though she never committed herself to any particular religion.

Partly as a result of the spiritual and emotional crisis she was undergoing, Helen's health collapsed and work became impossible. She was retired from the Treasury on health grounds and given a pension. Released from the source of some of her questioning, Helen began the process of piecing her life back together. She became involved in a consultancy role in 'business in the community' and, through this new area of work, found some of her ethical dilemmas were resolved.

It was round about this time that Eleanor, Helen's mum, was diagnosed as suffering from Alzheimer's disease. The days when her parents made frequent visits to London to stay with Helen, and her brother and sister, abruptly ended. The children made time to visit home as often as other commitments allowed, but Charles, Helen's dad, was left bearing a lonely burden of caring for a sick wife. He coped admirably for three years until she died in 1987, a year after Helen's retirement from the Civil Service.

Six months after losing his wife, Charles was just about managing to cope again with life, when fate dealt a second blow. Out driving in his car, he was involved in a serious accident. He sustained multiple injuries. When doctors claimed he was making a good and speedy recovery, his three children sensed something was amiss. Medical staff dismissed his sometimes odd behaviour as inevitable in a man in his early 80s, but the children had first-hand experience of dementia in older people, and they sensed it was not what their dad was suffering. They spent four frustrating months attempting to engage appropriate therapy for Charles, but to no avail. The care he was given consisted of treatment on psycho-geriatric hospital wards. He was frequently given sedation if he showed signs of aggression.

The matter was brought to a head during a holiday Charles spent with Jenny, his eldest daughter, and his son Mark, and each of their families. One day they were out sight-seeing in Norfolk when Charles suddenly collapsed. He was rushed to hospital in Norwich and later transferred to Addenbrokes Hospital in Cambridge, where it transpired that, ever since his car accident, Charles' brain had been bleeding internally. At last, here was vindication of their anxieties. The three children were placed in a difficult position: how to care for an elderly man from Northumbria, in hospital in Cambridge, when they each lived in London.

It was decided that the most therapeutic environment for Charles would be his own home up in Northumbria. Jenny and Helen set about organising a rota of care between themselves. Each weekend, they would scarcely have opportunity to talk for a few minutes, before exchanging places at their father's side. The constant travelling, involving hundreds of miles each journey, began to take its toll, however, and attempts were made to find alternative paid care in the home. Their efforts were proving fruitless, when, one weekend, the support of all three alternating paid carers fell through. Helen was left desperately trying to find a long-term solution.

She decided to find emergency help for a few days, long enough to allow her to wind up her affairs back in London and move in with her dad for the foreseeable future, Jenny by this stage being completely worn out.

With her intellectual background, Helen set about reading and learning all she could about head injuries. The physiological damage to her dad was obvious; there was ample evidence pointing to the effects of the injury. The main difficulty her father encountered was in finding the words to express what he wanted to say. Many of his attempts to speak sounded like confused nonsense. The confusion extended to basic living tasks. He could no longer recall how to complete household jobs. Additionally, his injuries had removed his inhibitions. In ways totally out of character, he would insult people in public, or speak in lewd terms.

Unbeknown to herself, Helen hit upon a strategy for helping her dad which was being pioneered at the time by doctors of head-injured patients. Her therapy was to deal with the problems piecemeal. She identified all the small processes with which her father had difficulties and worked out methods of helping him conquer them. She developed a detailed routine to which he adhered day by day, to build up his ability in all the areas where he had lost out.

An example of this would be getting breakfast. Each night Helen set out the items required to make porridge in exactly the same positions. When her father came down to the kitchen the next morning, she would stand behind him, giving instruction, correcting mistakes, though not in a negative fashion (not, for instance, by saying 'don't do it like that'), but in a positive manner (for example, saying 'pick up the wooden spoon'). Gradually, in the months in which she became the 'worker', the 'therapist', which she had failed to find elsewhere, Charles relearned most of the tasks he had lost the ability to perform.

When he was 95 per cent recovered, Helen felt it was time to begin confronting some of the emotional and psychological problems Charles faced. It was at this stage that Jenny began to show outward anxiety about the methods Helen was using to help her dad. Fundamentally, the two sisters are very different and theirs was a history of failure to understand each other's outlook on life. Helen describes her sister as a natural 'motherer'. While Helen was giving emotional support to her father, however, hers was a very different approach to his needs from the one preferred by Jenny. Jenny wished to protect her father, while Helen wanted to 'work' with him as a means towards recovery. It pained Jenny to witness her father's distress, brought about by Helen's confrontation with his emotional and psychological scars. Eventually, Jenny's discomfort became too much for her to bear and she initiated a heated debate with her sister.

The two failed to resolve their difficulties. Mark, too, had deep-rooted problems relating to his sisters, on top of which his wife had just miscarried in their final attempt at pregnancy, so that he felt in no position to act as arbiter, and withdrew. The end result was that Helen left in disgust and the two went their separate ways.

Now Charles was the responsibility of Jenny and she felt the only viable long-term solution to finding care for him was to seek residential care. The sisters are now on speaking terms, though their relationship is very strained. Helen still bitterly regrets Jenny's decision to find a home for their dad. She maintains that almost all the hard-won progress achieved in helping Charles back to independence has been lost. She attributes this to the stress of living in a communal environment. Head-injured patients have reduced brain capacity, so that stress has deleterious effects upon their health. She considers herself to be an expert in her father's condition and is, thus, doubly frustrated that the staff in the home, good though it is, never listen to her recommendations for his care. She feels they perceive the interest she shows as nagging, and that they resent being told how to do their job. Once again, her ideas are met with cries of, 'What can you expect in someone his age?' No one but her brother and sister agrees with her that his symptoms are of head injury and not of other conditions associated with old age.

The experience of caring for her dad has had profound consequences upon Helen's life. It is now a year since she cared full-time for her dad, but she is still constantly exhausted. She can find no energy left to work and even has problems motivating herself to get up in the morning. Added to this apathy and lethargy are very real financial deficits brought about by caring for her dad. Long-distance phone calls with professionals, lengthy journeys home and the loss of earnings have whittled down all her savings, so that she now lives on a knife-edge, surviving on her pension. Perhaps the greatest damage, though, has been done to Helen's emotions. She regrets that no paid worker helped her and her brother and sister to work through their differences and reach considered, mutually acceptable solutions to the problem they faced in finding care for their dad. Instead, the stress of the situation brought past tensions to the surface of their relationships and caused them to say and do hurtful things to one another.

Before she became involved in caring full-time for her dad, Helen was aware of these problems mounting between herself and her siblings and tried to find emotional support. The counsellor she saw, however, in many ways did more harm than good by taking a very active approach and asking Helen to work at aspects of the relationships. In the throes of a demanding, traumatic situation, Helen lacked the emotional reserves with which to deal with her problems and the counselling agreement broke down. Headway, the voluntary organisation representing head-injured people and their relatives, stood out as by far and away the most useful source of help, but their support was of a very practical nature. Helen needed emotional support, but not of the kind provided by her counsellor. She merely wanted someone's shoulder on which to cry, as she puts it.

While she was looking after her dad, Helen became involved with a couple of the local churches. She had to take her dad along to the Plymouth Brethren and in so doing recognised some of the more positive aspects of the Christian faith. While she saw some of their beliefs as primitively naïve, she respected the ordinary folk who belonged to the chapel in their sincere faith. She was also impressed by the practical Christianity shown by the Methodist church in the village in which she lived. They provided a social setting with great therapeutic value for her father, in the day centre for old people which they ran. They also gave Helen considerable practical and emotional support.

Since her return to London, Helen has attended meetings of both a local Anglican church, and a central London Anglican church which has embraced a more radical, less mainstream philosophy. She feels she has a long way yet to go on her spiritual pilgrimage, but finds many of the ideas of these two churches very satisfying. Both are helping ease her back into London life.

The future is a blank for Helen. She can live only by taking one day at a time and even then sometimes reaches rock bottom. She feels lonely and is very sad that her relationships with her relatives are going through such a poor patch. She would dearly love to write her ideas on the needs of head-injured people into a book for families and professionals. In particular, she feels the need to make use of every opportunity to get over to professional people that the views of relatives of head-injured patients count for a lot. To this end, she has spoken at a number of conferences.

Most demoralising of all for Helen is the sense that the benefit of all her endeavours to help her father have been wasted. She grieves to see him in a condition almost as bad as it was before she began helping him. The future for him, as she sees it, is uncertain, and she feels helpless to affect it.

References

1. Brenda Baalham, *One in a Million*, Lutterworth Press, 1991.
2. Nancy Kohner, *Caring at Home; A Handbook for People Looking After Somebody at Home*, King's Fund, 1988.
Jane Brotchie, *Help at Hand; The Home Carer's Survival Guide*, Bedford Square Press, 1990.
3. Pat Saunders, *The A–Z of Disability; Directory of Information, Services, Organisations, Equipment and Manufacturers*, The Crowood Press, 1989.

6. A prisoner in my own home

Pauline wants to write a book about her life. She knows what she would call it; the title would be 'Say Hello, Mandy!' Thinking back on my conversation with Pauline, I could easily believe I imagined it. That someone should endure a life of such hardship is beyond comprehension.

Pauline says caring is a full-time job, except that she will never retire and receive a pension, and no one will give her a medal for long service. She had no 'apprenticeship' but, over the years, has become a qualified nurse, a mental health visitor, a cleaner, a secretary . . . She told me that it is just as well she does it for love, not money. She knows she has saved the government a small fortune in residential care fees, and receives for her endeavours a few pounds' 'wages' a day. After many years caring, she was allocated a social worker. On her first visit, the social worker asked, 'Do you work?' In that question, Pauline recognised the incomprehension of those around her of the role she fulfilled.

Pauline and her husband, Jack, were the only people who welcomed Mandy into the world. They had married three years earlier, when Pauline was 17 and pregnant. Her parents had been ashamed at the birth of their first grandchild, Peter, and had greeted Mandy's birth with no pleasure, following so quickly on the heels of her brother's birth.

As she watched her little girl develop, Pauline was not happy. She did not make the progress which Pauline had witnessed in Peter. She had convulsions. Her eyes seemed to have a strange stare and would appear to pop out of her face from time to time. The family GP dismissed Pauline's anxieties as the groundless worries of a very young mother. At a few months of age, however, Mandy had a huge convulsion. She was rushed to hospital and within minutes was diagnosed as suffering a massive brain tumour behind the eyes.

At just 20, Pauline waited helplessly as doctors at Great Ormond Street Hospital operated to remove part of the tumour. She then had to take the baby to the Royal Marsden Hospital for radium treatment, leaving her son with relatives, whilst she struggled on public transport to unknown places. Only her deep love for her child enabled her to find the courage to face those traumatic events. When Mandy had received all the treatment her body could withstand in a lifetime, she was sent home to her parents, who were told to bring her back in a year's time, if she survived.

During the following months and years, many were the occasions when Pauline and Jack feared Mandy would not live through the night. Their thin-walled council house was inadequate to shield the child against the rigours of one painfully cold winter. Ice formed under Mandy's bed. Poverty-stricken, Jack and Pauline took rugs from the floor to give their children extra warmth at night. Gradually, though, the hopelessness instilled by medical professionals began to lift. The family were neglected by their GP, who had not come to terms with the mistake he made, but they survived. As Pauline avidly watched the little girl playing, she noticed improvement. She was overjoyed one day to realise that Mandy's sight, lost during surgery, had returned. The fits remained, the tumour was still there, but the child's health was progressing. Time alone would reveal the severity of Mandy's residual handicap. It became apparent after a while that brain damage had been severe. Speech never came. She was in nappies until the age of six. But she was dearly loved by both her parents.

It was six years later, and once more to the disapproval of her parents, that Pauline conceived again. Despite Pauline's fears Kevin, her third child, was a healthy baby. The family GP made sure that he was examined very thoroughly to put at rest the minds of his parents. Three years later, Pauline and Jack's youngest child, Penny, was born.

Tragedy hit the family shortly after Penny's birth. Pauline's father, to whom she was very close, was killed in a road accident. He was just 57. Scarcely had Pauline recovered from the loss when, a year later, she was dealt a second bitter blow. Jack was preparing to go into business in the building trade with his cousin. In the meantime he had taken a temporary job delivering straw, to tide the family over. But on the day he resigned from this job, he had an accident which was to prove fatal. He fell from a lorry and broke his neck. Pauline left the children with their grandmother to spend four weeks with Jack at Stoke Mandeville Hospital.

During the daytime she would be with him, holding the newspaper for him to read while he lay helpless, surrounded by photographs of the children to whom he was so devoted. During the nights, Pauline slept in an eery room used as a bank during the day, on call for the many occasions when Jack seemed to be slipping away. After four grim weeks he died. Pauline returned, with the body of her husband, to her four children. She was a widow at 30, with a son of 13, a handicapped daughter of 11, a three-year-old son and a 14-month-old baby girl.

She managed as best she could, retreating to the solace of her mum's home during school holidays. Money was extremely scarce, so that she ate only leftovers after feeding the children. For birthdays, she could afford for them only a small box of cheap chocolates. She would turn up the radio when ice-cream vans passed near the house, so the children could not hear them. The family became very close. Her brothers and sister became protective of Mandy. They were obedient children, Pauline keeping a firm hand over them as they grew up; each would be in bed each night, she recalls, while school friends were still playing outside.

Within just a few years of her widowhood, however, Pauline lost her mum, the person upon whom she had relied for support. The day after she and the children had left her mum's home, one school holiday, the older lady collapsed and died of a heart attack. She was in her early 60s. Finally, if Pauline believed life could throw at her no further disasters, she was wrong. Before long, her only sister was to fall ill with cancer at the age of 47. Pauline became her nurse, tending the dying woman and caring for her sister's family as well as her own. The illness reduced Pauline's sister to a skeleton before finally taking her life, two years later. Pauline was alone in the world. She had only her four children for comfort and company.

At the age of seven, Mandy had started attending a club on Friday afternoons. She then moved on to a special school during the week, until she was 16. She was heavily dependent on Pauline for her mental age was judged to be a mere two and a half years. It was not possible, therefore, for Pauline to be in regular paid employment, but from time to time she picked strawberries or did a little cleaning to earn some extra money for the family.

Those years were very hard, but Pauline looks back on them with fond memories. She remembers the times when she took all four children on camping holidays, exploring, in their very old car, unknown parts of the country. Eight years after losing her husband, Pauline remarried. Tony, several years her senior, was a bachelor. Pauline's mum had warned her not to marry, fearing few men would possess the resources to take on the family. Tony proved himself to be more than equal to the task of caring for not only a severely handicapped stepdaughter, but three other children with adolescent needs. Fifteen years later, Pauline and Tony are still happily married. Tony does manual work for the local council, while Pauline has to be at home for Mandy. They have several grandchildren, as Peter, Kevin and Penny are all happily married themselves. Pauline is proud of the three of them. She feels the hardship of their early years has produced in them a kindness and a resourcefulness.

When Mandy left school at 16, she spent a while at a local training centre of which Pauline did not think highly. She is relieved that Mandy now, at the age of 34, is established in a day centre, which she considers to be very beneficial. Mandy spends the hours between 9.15 am and 4.00 pm at the centre. During those hours, Pauline shops and does housework, ever mindful of the clock, knowing, like Cinderella, she must be back by a certain time. Mandy cannot be left at all, so Pauline supervises her constantly. She spends her time playing with toys and her speech is restricted to a few inarticulate words. Pauline says they have their own language, which enables Mandy to communicate her needs.

Although Mandy can feed herself, she needs dressing and taking to the toilet. She cannot sit still on visits to the toilet, so Pauline frequently needs to clean both her daughter and the bathroom afterwards. Mandy has frequent fits, for which she is under medication. They are particularly common during her periods and cause her to become disorientated and sometimes violent. On occasions, fits happen when Mandy is out shopping with her mum, which has produced some embarrassing situations. The fits can be triggered by a number of circumstances, such as bright lights, extreme heat and cold temperatures.

The fits are the only symptom of the tumour Mandy still has. Pauline has long since given up believing she will outlive her daughter. She hopes for a long life, so she can go on caring for Mandy for many years to come, but she has hunted for a residential home for mentally handicapped people where she feels Mandy would be happy if she herself dies. She is adamant that her other three children must be saved the responsibility of caring for Mandy which has so dominated her own life. On the other hand, she feels her life would be empty if Mandy died, because her daughter is so much a part of her life. She remembers scarcely anything of her life before Mandy's birth, but every detail of Mandy's own life history is indelibly printed on her mind.

On the rare occasions when Tony and Pauline spend an evening out together, they have to use a skilled sitter who understands Mandy's condition. Even then, Pauline has to give detailed instructions, worries about Mandy all evening, and has to be back by a certain time. It means nights out are extremely rare.

Pauline has few friends of her own age. She has little opportunity to meet people and her peers seem to have such a different existence. She cannot imagine, for instance, what they do with their evenings. Even other carers are not on her wavelength, because few have cared for as long as she has. She says, though, that meeting them, in the carers support group she joined a couple of years ago, has given her an identity (she now calls herself a carer) and shown her how to assert her needs.

Occasionally she thinks longingly of the freedom she has never known. But any resentment that begins to surface is pushed under by compassion for her daughter whose life, she feels, has been affected by her disability to a far greater degree. She appreciates the small pleasures in life, like taking a long walk, with Mandy by her side, through the countryside around their village home. Her life has been filled with such trauma that, she says, she is pleased when life appears boring! Occasional breaks in the family caravan, with Tony and Mandy, are the nearest thing to respite care she knows, but she would not want it any other way. Caring for her 'little girl' seems to be the driving force in Pauline's life.

The restrictions carers face

In many ways, the aspect of caring which we discuss in this chapter overlaps with the information given in previous chapters. Certainly, some of the suggestions I shall make towards the end of the chapter will reflect those found earlier in the book.

A tale I heard today about one carer illustrates the very real 'imprisonment' many others face. She has a husband in the advanced stages of multiple sclerosis. Yesterday, while shopping, she bumped into a friend from church. She explained that she had snatched an opportunity, while her husband was sleeping, to dash to the shops for the groceries she needed. She had been hoping, she confessed, not to bump into anyone she knew, so pressed was she for time. On meeting her church friend, however, she spent an hour on the street, pouring out her feelings, while the kind friend stood and listened.

This was clearly a lady who, for all sorts of practical and emotional reasons, needed time away from her home, but was unable to find it. Her story is not unusual. There are a number of reasons why carers become tied to their homes. The first set are to do with the limitations of the help available to them. The second set are concerned with the carer's own attitudes and those of other members of the household.

Respite opportunities for carers

We saw, in chapter 5, that some of the services provided by the statutory, voluntary and private sectors are aimed at giving a break, some 'respite', as it is known, to carers. Some of these services, such as sitting services, family placement schemes, and care attendant schemes, give a carer a few hours' break, perhaps on a regular weekly basis. Other services do this as an indirect consequence of their activity. For instance, special schools, day centres and luncheon clubs are aimed at giving stimulation to disabled people, but have the benefit of giving their carers time off. Other services offer to carers longer breaks. Some residential homes, for example for frail elderly people, have beds set aside for short-term residents. In this way, a carer may have the chance to have a couple of weeks away from their loved one every few months. Of course, if the home is owned by a private company, there may be a fee involved. Hospitals, too, will very often have respite beds. Where carers are looking after terminally ill patients, hospices may fulfil this function.

Many carers rely on relatives to take over from them from time to time. I hear carers of elderly parents speak gratefully of the role of their husband, brother or sister, or sometimes even their children, in stepping in and taking over for a while from time to time.

The ways in which carers may use this time off varies considerably. For some, it is a chance to catch up on lost sleep, to rest and relax in their own homes. For others, it gives them time to do chores that would otherwise be difficult, such as gardening and shopping. For yet others, it gives the option of meeting up with friends, pursuing hobbies, spending an evening at the cinema. During longer breaks, other carers will go away on holiday.

Unfortunately, options for taking breaks are not limitless. Many carers report extreme difficulty finding a bed in a hospital or residential home. Many families compete for a seemingly ever-dwindling supply of respite places. The availability of day centres, sitting services and luncheon clubs varies from area to area, since many are the initiative of independent voluntary groups whose funding is, in any case, insecure. Given the existence of a service, it is no guarantee that carers will find out about it. By virtue of their 'housebound' way of life, it is difficult to target them with publicity. Problems in advertising services are compounded for those attempting to meet the needs of carers from ethnic minority communities, who may speak a different language and not share communal facilities with the wider society.

Many carers have little, or no, help from relatives. The situation of carers with no brothers or sisters can be particularly grim. We saw in chapter 2 how Sarah wishes she had a brother or sister with whom to share the care of her clinically depressed mum. Some carers find that relatives live too far away to offer viable support. In other cases, members of the extended family seem to assume that the carer can, and wants to, cope unaided and exempt themselves from sharing the care given to sick or disabled relatives.

In objective terms, therefore, respite and relief for carers is scarce. Funds are limited for supplying care at a national level and carers are not the highest priority of statutory agencies.

Attitudes limiting respite

In other, more subjective ways, however, opportunities for carers to take time off are circumscribed. This has to do both with their own attitudes and with the dynamics within the caring relationship and the wider household.

Turning to the attitudes of carers, many simply do not think to take a break from caring. They do not see themselves as a 'carer', but rather as the mother of their child, the husband of their wife, the daughter of their father. The concept of having 'time off' is, thus, alien. They can never cease to be their child's mother, their wife's husband, their father's daughter. However stressed and tired they may feel, to spend time away from their ailing relative does not enter their consciousness. It might even be construed by the carer as a rejection, an abandonment, of someone very dear who needs their constant presence. In offering carers a break, then, it is essential for providers of respite to encourage them to see their need to rest as legitimate. For some, it is a case of recognising that, if they do not have time off, their services will not be available to their relative for an indefinite period.

Some carers feel they would be at a loose end without their disabled loved one. Pauline, who we met earlier in this chapter, has no desire to be apart from her daughter, Mandy. An outing, or holiday, without Mandy would seem strange and unpleasant. Tom, in chapter 2, had the chance to go on holiday while his wife spent a fortnight in hospital, but he had no heart to go away and leave her. Where would he have gone, and with whom?

Very often, carers decline to use services that are on offer to them. They may feel that the options open to them do not suit their particular needs. Perhaps they would like help in the evenings, but services are available only during the day. Maybe they would prefer their relative to be taken out, but the help available is only offered in their own home. Problems can arise for carers from minority communities in our country. It is unacceptable for some of these carers to leave their disabled relative in a form of care which does not observe their cultural practices, be they dietary, religious, or of any other nature.

Another factor deterring carers from using respite services is the memory of unfortunate experiences in the past. They may feel that the residential home where their father spent a fortnight last summer did not meet the standards of the care they could have given him at home. Were they to leave him there again, they would spend all their time away from him worrying about his welfare. The 'stand in' carers do not understand how their relative prefers to be cared for, they feel, neglecting small aspects of hygiene and comfort to which they are attentive. In some extreme cases, they may even have returned from holiday to discover that their relative had been injured in some way, or that their condition had deteriorated while in respite care.

Thus we move on to probably the most significant reason behind a carer's failure to take time off; they feel guilty. Their relative has perhaps suffered while in care temporarily. Equally significant, their loved one may have pleaded with them, attempting to dissuade the carer from leaving them. The disabled person is aware that, in the care of others, they will not be looked after in the same way as they are at home. They may be embarrassed by the thought of a stranger caring for them. They may argue outwardly against separation from their carer. More often, however, a hurt glance, a stray tear, the averted look, all signal that, by taking time off, the carer is causing pain to their loved one.

A further element to their guilt is the frequent sense that other family members should not be burdened with demands for help. Many carers shield their relatives from caring responsibilities, which they see as their own exclusive preserve.

In terms of the negative attitudes of carers towards taking time off, two further points are worthy of mention. Firstly, many carers are simply so busy that they never find time to organise a break. It seems to require too much effort to make the necessary arrangements. Secondly, because there is sometimes expense involved, time off can appear to be an investment not worthy making, a luxury which they can do without. Others are too poor even to afford to pay.

The effects of unbroken caring

The consequence of this inability or unwillingness to take breaks is that many carers suffer perpetual exhaustion. As Christians, we recognise the message of the sabbath principle in the Bible. Human beings need to rest regularly from their labours in order to regenerate themselves. Caring is no less an occupation than many paid jobs, so that rest-times are as important for carers as they are for paid workers.

Pauline, whose story is found earlier in this chapter, has made a career out of caring. Caring has not been for her a short-term commitment. So far, it has absorbed over 30 years of her life. For 30 years and more she has cared at home for an extremely dependent child. Taking an occasional evening out is a near impossibility, requiring the strategic planning of a military operation. Neither does she have holidays away from her daughter, because to do so would be unusual and unpleasant.

We shall see later in the chapter that Sonia, who cares for her 36-year-old daughter, Jasmine, faces a situation very similar to Pauline's. She has been caring for well over 30 years, has no holidays away from home and finds that planning as much as a day out proves difficult because of the unpredictability of Jasmine's moods.

Pauline recognises that she is fortunate. She has good health. She knows that for other carers, like Sonia, good health is by no means guaranteed. Carers like Sonia all too often face illness and injury. They are constantly tired. As a result they often find that their mental health breaks down. They frequently have neither time nor inclination to recover adequately from their own health problems before being thrust back into the demands of caring. Many carers are themselves elderly and therefore prone to physical decline and diminishing energy.

Not only does the absence of adequate breaks affect health and morale, it also has a damaging impact upon a carer's relationships. Within the home, their relationship with the person for whom they are caring can become fractious and bad tempered when the two are thrust together for abnormally long periods of time. Sustaining relationships outside the carer's household can prove difficult too if the carer can never spend time away from the home. Outside interests, hobbies and paid work for instance, suffer as well, as the carer's time is monopolised by the demands of caring.

All too easily, a carer's life can become very narrow, as they become increasingly confined to their own home. Interaction with the wider world is reduced, friends drift apart.

Sonia comes from Jamaica. She left her native land at the age of 25;

married for seven years by then, she was the mother of three young children. Work was so scarce that Ian, her husband, was unable to find a job. Like many more before them, the couple believed that emigration to the UK might solve their financial worries. They decided to join an uncle of Sonia's who had moved over to a city in England some years before.

Ian and Sonia's eldest daughter, Jasmine, stayed in Jamaica with her grandmother for several years. Sonia had trained as a nurse and conceived a fourth child before little Jasmine joined the family in England at 10 years of age. It was only when she saw doctors in this country that problems of which Ian and Sonia had been aware for some time were diagnosed. Jasmine had been brain damaged at birth, which meant that her physical and mental development had been stunted.

Even now, at 36, Jasmine has tiny feet and is very small, with a hunched back, so that she is unable to walk very far. Although she can talk, her conversation is like that of a small child. She likes to play with toys and has a large collection of toy cars. Often Jasmine has unaccountable moods. For seemingly no reason she will cry and refuse to do what Sonia asks of her. She is incontinent and is unfortunately able to take off the pads she uses, so that Sonia is accustomed to finding her wet through from time to time. She is a restless person, and wanders around her parents' home, often trying to get out into the road. Her agitation manifests itself in poor sleeping patterns; Sonia says ruefully that none of the drugs designed to calm Jasmine down seem to have had long-term effectiveness.

For a great many years, Sonia managed to sustain a full-time job as a nurse, while raising four children, one of whom was severely disabled. She frankly admits that she can now scarcely believe that she managed to cope. She fitted in her hours as a nurse around Ian's job as a lorry driver. Mostly he worked days, so that she would be on night shifts. She would return each morning from a night on the wards of the local hospital ready to get the children out to school, before snatching a few hours sleep and waking in time to collect the children and keep up with housework. She realises now that she scarcely ever enjoyed long, refreshing hours of sleep.

By the time Sonia reached 49 years of age she was beginning to count the cost of the years of stress and pressure. She enjoyed her work very much and felt fulfilled in the role of caring for her sick patients, but she seemed always to feel exhausted. She wondered how long she would be able to sustain full-time employment. She had been asking questions about the future for only a short time when decisions were taken out of her hands. Sonia fell seriously ill.

She was told by doctors that she had a massive brain tumour and that she would need surgery very soon. She was warned that, following the operation, she might never walk again. She thought about how much Jasmine needed her and with fear, but trusting God, she went into hospital for the operation. It proved to be a very difficult piece of surgery, but was miraculously successful. Sonia's health is fragile, her strength is gone, but she thanks God that the only remaining permanent signs to remind her of her ordeal are a few scarcely noticeable marks on her head.

It was clear that Sonia could not return to work. What also became evident was that her stamina would not extend to caring for Jasmine full-time. Sonia and Ian have never talked explicitly with their two daughters, Angela who is 32, and Agatha, now 25 years old, about obligations within families. Somehow the two, as well as their 34-year-old brother Eric, have grown up with family values identical to those of their parents. Sonia explained to me that, where she comes from, people feel an unquestioning sense of loyalty towards their relatives. To hand over disabled children to be cared for by people outside the family would be unthinkable.

The family have, therefore, reached an arrangement whereby the two daughters, Agatha and Angela, share the work involved in caring for Jasmine with their ageing parents. Angela lives with Ian, Sonia and Jasmine, in the house the family own. She was working full-time as a nurse for a while, but made the decision to devote more time to caring for Jasmine, so that she now works only Saturdays and Sundays. Agatha works in the Civil Service, but spends her weekends at home, caring for Jasmine, to enable her mum and dad to get out to church.

Ian and Sonia have been going along to the church for 14 years altogether. Although she was raised in a Christian home, Sonia did not become actively involved in church life until she reached her fortieth birthday. She remembers how, in the early days, it was a struggle to keep up attendance at church. Living with the twin demands of working and caring for a disabled child, it was tempting some Sundays to stay at home and rest. But it was not long before Sonia realised that it was from her faith that she was drawing the strength she needed to continue carrying her heavy load. She is very grateful to her children who, over the years, have faithfully looked after Jasmine during church services.

Sonia's is a trusting faith. She acknowledges that many of her experiences would have led others to doubt the presence and the love of God. But she has always been able to believe that God knows best. From time to time she feels very low, but the despair rarely lasts long. Through constant prayer and a strong faith, she soon feels assured once more that God will supply the strength she needs to carry on caring for Jasmine.

Sonia is thankful for the encouragement she receives from fellow Christians at church. Most share her cultural background, so that they understand her outlook on life. They frequently express concern, asking questions about Jasmine and assuring Sonia of their prayers in ways that invariably succeed in lifting her spirits. On occasions, members of the congregation have looked after Jasmine. For instance, during family weddings to which Sonia, Ian, Eric, Angela and Agatha are invited, friends take care of Jasmine.

Caring for Jasmine places enormous restrictions upon Sonia's life. Planning ahead is impossible. Because Jasmine is prone to moodiness, Sonia can never know from one day to the next whether or not she will agree to go to the training centre she is supposed to attend from Monday to Friday. Sometimes, for no apparent reason, she lies down in the street screaming and refusing to be placed in the ambulance which transports her to the training centre. Consequently, to arrange a day out would be unwise, because of the risk that Sonia might need to stay at home with Jasmine.

Even something as straightforward as shopping presents difficulties for Sonia. Jasmine cannot walk far, but even if she did possess the resilience to do so, she would not have the inclination to accompany Sonia on long shopping expeditions. She gets bored after a few minutes and begs her mum to take her home. This means that Sonia must always be sure that someone is at home to look after Jasmine while she collects groceries. It also follows that Jasmine's clothes must be bought before they have been tried for size. Fortunately some of the local shops recognise Sonia's special circumstances and are happy for her to return or exchange goods that do not fit Jasmine, or meet with her approval.

If going shopping is troublesome, it comes as no surprise that taking holidays is completely unfeasible for the family. As a result, Sonia has only once returned to Jamaica. While she enjoyed her visit, she was ever conscious of the home situation, where her daughters were coping with Jasmine. She knows only too well that, were she able to spend breaks with her husband, she would merely feel guilty for burdening her daughters and spend the time away worrying about Jasmine.

Sonia complains about very little, but she feels she has been let down by local services. She has had a social worker for only a third of Jasmine's life. She was assigned a social worker only after persistent demands made by a nursing colleague. When her many telephone calls seemed to fall on deaf ears, this friend went to the Social Services department in person to secure for Sonia the help she could see she so desperately needed. Little changed, however, as a result of the social worker's intervention. Sonia was very rarely visited. It was only following her brain tumour that professionals seemed to realise that their help was required.

The family have not been saved from the effects of economic recession. Ian and Eric are both finding that their labour is not needed. Eric gets through by doing odd jobs. Ian does whatever driving he can find, but discovers that, in job interviews for stable posts, he is rejected in favour of younger men.

Sonia prays that she and Ian will remain well enough to be fully involved in caring for Jasmine for many years to come. She does not worry about Jasmine's future, though. She knows God has her daughter's best interests at heart. She is also happy in the awareness that Agatha, Angela and Eric are all devoted to the older sister. Their sense of commitment to Jasmine remains as strong as ever, strong enough for them to be willing to limit their independence, their leisure time and their employment prospects to care for her. She feels sure that Jasmine will never need to live in residential care.

Sonia feels that caring for Jasmine is harder than caring for a young child. With a young child, at least you know as a parent that one day your daughter will be independent. Jasmine's dependence is permanent. Also, a child is far more likely to respond to instruction than Jasmine is. But Sonia never wastes her energy dreaming of how life could have been. Jasmine is her daughter; she loves her dearly and cannot imagine life without her. From day to day, she draws strength from her faith and her family. Looking back over the time she has spent in England, it is a wonder to her that she found the perseverance to endure a life of enormous stress all those years. She realises even now that Jasmine's care is more than a full-time job, such that it taxes the energies of both part-time carers, Angela and herself. She has come to accept her situation, however, to the extent that she does not wish her life was otherwise.

Ways of helping carers take breaks

We have seen how many carers are deterred from using respite services because they do not appear to meet their individual needs. In finding ways of providing breaks for carers, therefore, we must make sure that we are sensitive to their specific requirements. Perhaps, therefore, you could come up with a few alternatives, and talk through with your carer friend which, if any, they would prefer.

Because many carers are reluctant to take breaks for fear of the effect this would have upon their dependent relative, we must also make sure that our suggestions benefit not only the carer, but the disabled person too. In this respect, we may have an advantage over other service providers, because we are known to the family, perhaps even a trusted friend; the disabled person may be less suspicious of us and our motives than they would be of a strange person.

It is, in fact, relatively easy, with thought and sensitivity, to devise ways of relieving carers which benefit their disabled relative too. For instance, many chronically sick people are lonely. They have few opportunities to mix with people outside their immediate family, particularly if they are housebound. In many cases they much appreciate friendly visitors who are concerned and interested.

Through showing friendship to the disabled person, we can sit with them of an evening from time to time, while the carer goes out to a church meeting. We need to be careful in our approach, however. We should be prepared not only to give of ourselves, but to receive blessing and encouragement from our disabled friend. In this way our friendship with them can be mutually enriching.

A carer like Pauline might particularly appreciate your offer to sit with their disabled relative if you possess skills in caring, either through a professional background in an area like nursing, or through having cared yourself for a disabled relative. Even if you are skilled and experienced, the carer may still want to give detailed instructions, for their own peace of mind, so try to listen humbly and attentively.

You may wish to offer the disabled person hospitality in your own home, or even to take them out for the day. A single lady who wrote to me recently said how grateful she would be if members of her church congregation offered to take her sister, who has cerebral palsy, out for a day trip. You and your carer friend will need to assess whether or not your house, and even your car, can accommodate easily the disability of the dependent person. Once again, you may need to listen carefully as your carer friend explains how to look after their loved one. Give them the opportunity to brief you in detail.

In all likelihood you will need to win the trust of the disabled person gradually. At first it may be appropriate for them to spend just a couple of hours at your home. As your friendship with them grows, they may then stay for overnight trips; eventually you may find they are willing to stay with you for several days. By this stage your carer friend will we hope be confident in your ability to take good care of their loved one!

Perhaps you feel your carer friend needs a holiday. There are ways in which you can help on this front too. If the carer would prefer to holiday with their disabled relative, you could buy the Royal Association for Disability and Rehabilitation's guide to holidays catering for disabled people which would give them ideas for finding suitable activities and accommodation.(1) It is available from most branches of W H Smith. If they feel that, to take an adequate rest, they would need to leave their disabled relative behind, perhaps you could help them explore local respite care opportunities. Finally, through accompanying the family yourself, you could help to make a holiday possible for them.

Another area to consider is the financing of respite care. If your carer friend has as income only the disability benefits available, they may not be able to afford to take a holiday away from home. Perhaps you could tactfully offer financial assistance or give an anonymous gift. There may even be a case for organising a collection amongst friends of the carer to pay for a holiday. This would not only serve the purpose of giving the carer a change of scene and, were they to stay in a hotel or guesthouse, a rest. It would also demonstrate to the carer that they are held in the thoughts and affections of those around them.

You could play a crucial part in allowing your carer friend to recognise that it is both legitimate and necessary to take a break from caring. Books like the pamphlet *Taking a Break* and the

Bedford Square Press guide *Help at Hand* might be of help in giving them both information and a sense that every carer deserves to rest regularly.(2) You may even have a role to play in helping the disabled person to see how important it is that their carer has time to relax.

In all sorts of ways, then, you could play an important part in giving the carer permission and opportunity to spend time resting and relaxing from week to week. In this way, you will help them to husband their strength and to remain in the role of carer for as long as they desire to do so. There may come a point when, no matter how often they take breaks, however, the carer may possess within themselves no more resources for coping. Your role at this stage could be crucial in allowing the carer to see that there is no disgrace in handing over the practical aspects of caring to someone better able to perform them. You will need to stress that caring does not end when a disabled person enters residential accommodation, hospital or a hospice. Rather, as you need to impress upon them, the important elements of the caring relationship which arise from two persons loving one another never cease. They may even be enriched after the carer has given up the stressful nursing tasks with which they have been struggling.

As ever, it will be your approach which will benefit the carer. So remember not to be heavy handed in the help you give. Overbearing advice will not aid the carer. Rather, you should be mindful always of the need to enable the carer to see what is best for them and make their own decisions about the nature and frequency of the breaks they will take in their caring role.

References

1. Royal Association for Disability and Rehabilitation, *Holidays in the British Isles; A Guide for Disabled People*, 1991.
2. *Taking a Break; a Guide for People Caring at Home*, Health Education Authority (available from the King's Fund), 1987.
Jane Brotchie, *Help at Hand; The Home Carer's Survival Guide*, Bedford Square Press, 1990.

7. Thinking big

CARELINK: Churches' concern for carers

Watford and District Association for Church Social Work (WADACSW) has a long and distinguished history. Established in 1900, it is an initiative of the Anglican churches of Watford and Rickmansworth, but is open to involvement from churches of all denominations. The composition of its executive reflects its interdenominational emphasis.

WADACSW had, as its first goal, the support of young girls who were either pregnant outside marriage or in trouble with the law. The unmarried mother and her baby continued to be the focus for over 70 years, until, in 1977, the state took responsibility for their needs. WADACSW then carried out a survey of local needs which revealed the need for an Alcohol Advice Centre. For ten years, thereafter, WADACSW developed an advice service to people with alcohol problems and their families. The service was so successful that in 1989 it became a charity in its own right, with backing from the local authority.

As in 1977, WADACSW was faced with the question: how do we best use our resources to serve our community? Their first step was to consult local groups to ascertain perceptions of local need. Contact with both statutory and voluntary agencies, and churches themselves, elicited a range of ideas, but one common theme to emerge was the needs of carers of elderly and disabled people. It was this category of people that the Association then decided to target.

The immediate task that WADACSW set itself was to circulate a survey questionnaire. Two thousand copies were given to professionals in the area, who were to hand them on to carers. The questions asked were an attempt to establish how carers perceived their own needs and the kinds of services they would prefer, in an attempt to meet those needs.

The second task which the committee considered to be essential was to appoint a researcher to carry out, if you like, a 'feasibility study'. Barbara Roberts, herself a highly qualified nurse, began working 10 hours a week in October 1989. Her role was to liaise with churches, health and social services personnel, caring organisations and carers. She was to assess existing services and identify outstanding needs, search for ideas for potential projects which could be sponsored by the Association, and present a report on her findings.

Barbara very quickly found that she was working beyond the 10 hours a week for which she was paid. Such was her commitment to the project underway, however, that she cheerfully bore with the extra demands on what was already an overcrowded timetable.

To Barbara's mind, an essential component of her role was to become fully conversant with the ideas about caring and carers' needs currently emanating both from contemporary research on the issue, and from groups representing or working with carers at a national level.

She looked at studies of informal caring, particularly the Supplement to the 1985 *General Household Survey* on the topic. She examined some of the causes behind the apparent invisibility of carers. She looked at charters which had been drawn up, setting down clear guidelines for meeting carers' needs. She studied other projects across the country that were attempting to meet carers' needs. She considered the special role that the voluntary sector, including the Church, can play in supplementing the work of other agencies. Finally, she examined the political and social context of WADACSW's initiative, concluding that the timing was right. Legislative initiatives on community care were emphasising the crucial role of carers, while new studies were revealing the great stress under which many carers were labouring.

At the same time as researching the role of carers on a wider scale, Barbara was taking steps towards establishing the peculiar needs of carers locally. In this respect, the first job was to analyse the results of the survey of carers mentioned earlier. Possibly because professionals had not distributed questionnaires as widely as had been anticipated, the response rate was low. Barbara had only 83 completed questionnaires to analyse. From the results, however, she was able to see that two-thirds of the carers who responded could only go out if someone were to sit with their dependent. Only half of all the carers benefited from day care and less than a third from respite care. Support was expressed for the idea of carers support groups and a drop-in centre in which to leave the dependent. The most popular suggestion, however, was the idea of a volunteer to sit with the dependent relative on a regular basis.

The second job which Barbara undertook, as a means of gauging the feelings of local carers, was to visit personally several of those who had returned questionnaires. Two-thirds of those of whom visits were requested replied in the affirmative, so that Barbara, in total, visited 14 carers. Her first observation was that many seemed grateful for the opportunity her visit afforded them to talk about their experiences. She was detained with many far beyond the hour no longer than which she had promised to stay.

Barbara realised, from her conversations with carers, that there were several areas in which WADACSW's help would be particularly appreciated. Support groups would have been welcomed by quite a number. Similarly, advice and information on carers' rights was a commonly expressed need. The suggestion that was greeted with universal support, however, was the provision of visitors who would become 'trusted friends'.

There was another avenue of investigation Barbara felt the need to pursue. She initiated discussion with professionals working within the fields of social services and the health sector. Social workers were rather circumspect in the encouragement they offered. They felt volunteers had a useful role to play but, to safeguard clients, their endeavours needed to be co-ordinated by a paid organiser responsible for training and supervision, they suggested.

Health personnel gave warmer endorsements of the potential for people in churches to provide practical help. It seemed to Barbara that they would offer referrals more willingly than the social workers she met. Meetings with local carers' groups (one a member of the Alzheimer's Disease Society, others attached to local churches) highlighted that the role of volunteers in relieving carers would be slightly ambiguous where the dependent person suffered particular conditions, especially mental illnesses.

The hospital chaplain who spoke to Barbara expressed the view that he would present WADACSW with an ideal referral point. Many individuals from local groups gave advice which Barbara says she found most useful. At a national level, the development officers of the Carers National Association helped in the development of ideas.

Last, but by no means least, to be consulted were the churches that made up WADACSW. Their support for suggestions was crucial if the project was to be developed. In the report on her research(1), Barbara expresses disappointment at the lack of response with which her enquiries met. Following the circulation of information on her research, feedback from churches was limited. They proffered muted backing for the plans, holding back on promising unconditional funding, though offering the use of their buildings in some cases, and reporting that no support groups existed for carers in their congregations.

Barbara decided to pay visits to leaders of five key churches to talk in depth about the options available. When asked whether future activity should be restricted to church members, or alternatively have a wider ambit, they opted for the latter. When asked if they thought volunteers would be forthcoming from their churches the response was equivocal.

After roughly a year's research, Barbara felt able to make recommendations to the Association. Her work had confirmed the appropriateness of their involvement with carers. Moreover, it seemed to point to the desirability of launching some sort of scheme, run by paid co-ordinators, to send trusted volunteers into the homes of carers to give them a break. While a befriending scheme would be a priority, however, further services, such as carers' support groups, would need to follow, it seemed. The scheme, it was felt, would be best targeted at this stage towards the carers of elderly people whose conditions were not mental.

At WADACSW's Annual General Meeting in May 1990, a proposal for a befriending scheme for carers and their elderly dependents was presented. It was recommended that the Association appoint two co-ordinators whose role would be to: raise awareness within churches of the need for the scheme; recruit volunteers and match them with carers and their dependent relatives; support volunteers; and provide information for volunteers and carers.

It was suggested that two part-time co-ordinators be appointed, with hours which overlapped to maximise co-operation. The office of WADACSW would be a base for the project and finances would be sought from the local authority, health and social service authorities and churches etc. To start with, the scheme would cover only a limited area. Co-ordinators, it was proposed, would have a support group to advise them. Future goals that were mentioned were setting up carers' support groups, providing a telephone/listening service and setting up a drop-in centre.

Church reps present at the AGM warmly supported the proposal for a befriending scheme for carers. They asked about the financing of the project and were told that the capital reserves of the Association would cover the payment of the two co-ordinators for the initial two years. The church reps then recommended that local authorities and trust funds be approached, anticipating that resources would also be available from churches, once the scheme was fully established.

Those present at the AGM felt, however, that before plans could proceed, member churches of WADACSW not present should be consulted. Barbara circulated all 52 churches with details of the proposal and 41 per cent responded. Though generally the response was supportive, several reservations were expressed. Some churches felt that the supply of volunteers would be small, some that there would be overlap with other services, others that there was little justification for focusing on elderly people.

Their reservations were considered. Barbara and her fellow committee members felt the focus on elderly people was legitimate, since they were the largest group of disabled people, and theirs were often the hidden carers. Doubts about the supply of volunteers were considered to be insufficient to delay the scheme and at the next quarterly WADACSW meeting, the scheme was 'christened' CARE-LINK: Churches' Concern for Carers, on the recommendation of the Committee. The goals were to be to provide: a friend to carers and their elderly relatives; an opportunity for the carer to get out; a listening ear for the carer and their relative; and help in practical ways.

A job description was then drawn up for potential co-ordinators and eventually two suitable candidates emerged who were willing to work 18 hours between them, overlapping slightly in working times. Their base is at the WADACSW office. WADACSW were keenly aware of the need to balance the advertising of the scheme with the supply of volunteers, so that clients would not be disappointed, and so that volunteers would not lose interest. The Committee were also certain that volunteers would require sufficient support and training (in areas such as listening skills, how to get help in emergencies and when to seek expert help), and individual contracts for each would be helpful in defining commitments.

The Committee felt the best means of recruiting volunteers would be by word of mouth and publicity in local churches, but agreed that references would need to be sought, to eliminate unsuitable volunteers. It was anticipated that volunteers would include a broad mix, and not necessarily be Christians, while accepting the Christian basis of the organisation. Perhaps the most likely source of volunteers, it was expected, would be active elderly people.

It was time to give some thought to the qualities which volunteers would need. They, it was felt, should include: an ability to listen; a friendly disposition; the ability to empathise; awareness of the need for confidentiality; the ability to cope in an emergency; a willingness to share concerns with a co-ordinator; and the ability to know when they are 'out of their depth' and to refer appropriately.

Each applicant, it was concluded, would be interviewed by a co-ordinator to fill in details not provided on their application form, to check out their motivation, to ensure they were familiar with the goals of CARELINK, and to clarify that, should they fail to give satisfaction to a client, they should be withdrawn from that case.

In most cases, it was felt, some training would be crucial before volunteers would be matched with carers. The kinds of things that would be included in training would be; knowledge of carers' needs; knowledge of the needs of elderly people; what to expect from a first meeting (for example, the carer's reluctance to 'let go'); listening skills; when to refer to the co-ordinator; the support available for carers; emergencies that might occur and how to deal with them; lifting skills; first aid; communication skills; and helping the bereaved.

The volunteers would be in regular contact with the co-ordinators, often at the initiative of the co-ordinator. A newsletter, it was felt, may give a sense of corporate identity to the scheme. Volunteers would be drawn from all walks of life, their travelling expenses paid by the scheme. Their opinions would be valued and solicited in the development of new services. Arrangements for insurance cover for them whilst in the homes of carers would be taken out on behalf on WADACSW.

In terms of overall support, a Support Group, drawn from the Executive Committee, but including also two people with expertise in this area of work, would help guide the project, though not restricting the freedom of co-ordinators. The latter would regularly feed back to the Support Group and write an Annual Report for the Association.

Finally, the Committee agreed to undertake ongoing evaluation, particularly of a qualitative nature, in order partly to give guidance to others considering similar initiatives.

Matters to consider

This book has been peppered with suggestions for helping carers, some small scale, others demanding considerable time, effort and commitment. What marks out ideas in previous chapters from ones to be found in this chapter is that they can be carried out by a concerned individual, acting upon their impulse to care, through their own resources.

The apparent inbalance between the formal and the informal, the small scale and the large scale, has been intentional. The rationale that has underpinned it concerns the unique role for which I believe the Church has potential.

The majority of organisations working with carers are organised and structured by nature. They provide financial benefits and services according to rules. They are mediated by structures. Individuals working within them are bound by certain codes and processes. It is this very 'organisation' which carers can find intimidating and unsatisfactory. Help can be difficult to enlist and, once enlisted, can appear rigid and inflexible. 'The day centre is not what mum needs, and I cannot plan my day because I do not know when she will be collected.' 'Help in the home is only available between 9.00 am and 5.00 pm, when I am at my most harrassed at 7.00 am and 8.00 pm.'

The help that churches provide is very different. Christians are not caring as a profession, but as an expression of their faith, we hope. The bulk of help that is given is spontaneous, if a church is functioning healthily. Churches have the capacity to embody the 'community' which the elusive policy of Care in the Community it is hoped will evoke. It is a 'body' of people bound by common hopes and beliefs; part of its *raison d'etre* is to meet each other's needs. It has been called a 'family' and in that respect it can offer to carers the flexible, sensitive support they so welcome from their own relatives and friends.

One proviso, however, must be added at this point. Only in the past decade has research in this country revealed the needs of carers. It would be unfair and unrealistic to expect individual Christians to possess, from their own experience of life, an accurate perception of carers needs. They must be equipped if they are to react sensitively. There are many ways to raise the awareness of church congregations regarding carers' needs: videos are available to be shown at meetings; many helpful books have been written; some carers are willing to talk to churches about their needs.(2) How about lending this book to friends?

There comes a time, however, when the Church, no matter how rich in personal caring, must face the need to formalise some of the help it can offer. This does not mean, however, that the unique flexibility and versatility of its response need be lost. It must be prized and cherished. Any scheme which becomes too large to be sensitive needs reconsidering.

Church-based schemes must be flexible in two respects. Firstly, each carer has a different set of needs. This book has attempted to highlight some of those needs, but each carer faces a unique blend and intensity of needs. Their experience of caring can be influenced by any number of factors. It varies according to their relationship with the person for whom they care. It is affected by the illness of the person, with mental problems perhaps inducing greater emotional, but fewer practical, problems. A final factor is geographical. Carers' needs reflect something of their environment. Though they share many concerns, the rural carer's situation will vary from the urban carer's.

A second reason for building flexibility into any church's caring programme stems from the nature of the church itself. It too will have unique resources and potential which will fluctuate with time. That is precisely why none of the ideas located in this chapter are hard and fast models for churches. They simply represent ways in which some churches have responded to carers needs, or guidelines for future responses. Each church must assess its potential. It must look carefully at the people who constitute the church and discern where their gifts lie. It should consider its infrastructure, examining opportunities for using its buildings, for instance. It should analyse its surrounding community to find which social needs are evident amongst local people.

All these considerations point to the need for careful research and investigation as a prerequisite for effective action. The most important piece of research to be carried out will be a survey of carers' needs. This can be undertaken in several ways. Churches have used questionnaires. They have also interviewed carers in the vicinity. They have spoken to local professional people. Each method has helped in pointing the way forward.

Another important piece of research involves contacting other local agencies. It is futile to set up a scheme which duplicates a service on offer from other sources. In the current climate, Social Services departments and health authorities cannot afford to ignore community groups such as churches, as we shall see later. Though professionals are sometimes reticent about engaging in partnerships with churches, in many areas churches have become trusted allies of health and social services workers, in the care of vulnerable people. I believe statutory agencies appreciate being consulted by community groups.

And so we move on to looking at the options open to churches as they embark upon a programme of reaching out to carers. At this stage of planning, it is helpful for churches to assess their capacity to operate on their own in providing a service. It might be that small projects are within the capability of single churches. Where ambitious schemes are underway, however, a partnership between several churches may be advisable. To be overstretched is to be vulnerable. It might be that the obvious partners for your initiative are not other churches, but local voluntary groups who share your concerns. Your enquiries might reveal, for instance, that the energies of your church fellowship would be best directed at supplementing the resources of a local Age Concern group. There may be opportunities for you to supply volunteers for a sitting service, drivers to transport carers to a support group, or buildings for the use of a drop-in centre for carers.

If all you decide to do is to make sure carers in the congregation are aware of the services available to them from other groups, you will be achieving something worthwhile. But even this role requires careful research, constant up-dating of information. A final piece of advice in helping carers is that you might like to consider how existing services provided by your churches might be extended to carers. Perhaps the church has a group providing practical help to elderly people, or trained counsellors. Could the services of these people be extended to carers?

The touchstone of any help offered to carers, be it individual or project-based, should be reliability. Many carers have become despairing of ever receiving support. If their expectations are low, at least then they do not run the risk of disappointment. To offer a glimmer of hope to such a carer immediately raises expectations. To fail to fulfil promises can be more hurtful than offering nothing in the first place. It is essential that churches are assured that they have the wherewithal to provide a service before they begin to publicise it, just as it is essential for individuals who promise to visit a carer to honour their commitment. Reliability and trustworthiness are key words. Nothing more dishonours the Church than broken promises.

Finally, we need to be careful in the ways in which we embark upon corporate ventures. For instance, we will undoubtedly need to look into the options for insuring volunteers against injury and accidents. The full legal implications of setting up a project, of using volunteers, of employing staff, of assuming charitable status, of deploying capital resources (such as buildings), of budgeting and book-keeping, need careful research. Help can be obtained from groups like your local Council for Voluntary Services and Volunteer Bureau, or equivalent.

Meeting the spiritual needs

The Church, unlike any other institution, exists to meet spiritual needs. Many carers have pressing spiritual concerns. They commonly question, as we saw in chapter 3, the love of God in situations where loved ones, and consequently they themselves, are suffering. The questions they ask are likely to be different from the ones you and I are asking. How then can they be answered?

An idea for meeting the spiritual needs of carers is to set up a Bible study group for them, a forum in which they can discuss spiritual issues which worry them. Just as young mums have special meetings to air their feelings and discuss spiritual issues pertinent to raising children, so carers could join up once a week, once a fortnight, or once a month, to toss around ideas, pray and study.

One issue which would need careful thought would be the care of their relative during meetings. There may be a case for those in the congregation with time to spare offering hospitality to the disabled person, or spending time at their own home, getting to know them. Another way in which members of the congregation could be involved is in inviting the group to meet in their home, unobtrusively supplying refreshments and a comfortable environment.

Carers, however, must not be separated out from the rest of the congregation. They must be integrated, their needs met through the ordinary course of church life. They share in common with the other Christians in their church a need for fellowship, for teaching, for worship, for social outlets. Yet for many carers maintaining church attendance can become overwhelmingly difficult. Sadly, their struggle to continue involvement with the fellowship is often unobserved.

A married couple, caring for a housebound 95-year-old mother, found that the only way they could sustain involvement in their village church was to alternate their attendance at services. They would take it in turns to stay with mum, while the other would pop out for an hour or two to the service. Unfortunately, no one in the church was perceptive enough to realise that they sorely missed being able to worship as a couple. So unaware was the church of their dilemma that one week they were both asked to read lessons on the same Sunday morning!

For this couple, the problem could so easily have been solved if members of the congregation had been willing to sacrifice their own attendance at church once in a while, to sit with mum while the couple enjoyed a morning together away from home, recharging their spiritual, social and emotional batteries.

Churches can so easily lose touch with carers. The carer's absence from services is initially remarked, and efforts are made to keep them informed of and involved in church life. But, as time passes, they fade from memory. It is, tragically, at the moment when such a carer feels most isolated and cut off from the world, that their church's neglect is most pronounced.

It would be helpful for churches to sit down with each of their carers and work out the most helpful way of keeping them involved in church life. There may be a case for reassessing the carer's level of commitment to the church, and relieving them of onerous responsibilities, so long as those responsibilities are not a vital link with life outside home. There may also be an opportunity to draw up a rota of people willing to sit with a housebound relative while the carer attends church meetings. Services could be taped for the benefit of carers unable to take part.

On another level, the church should ensure that its buildings are accessible for disabled people, so that a carer is able, if they should wish to, to bring along their disabled relative to meetings. In particular, seating arrangements should allow them to sit together in a situation which does not make their presence conspicuous.(3)

Finally, in order for the expression of faith found in the church to be as relevant and helpful as possible to carers and their disabled relatives, care is needed. The wording of prayers and songs, of sermons, should be framed in ways that do not exclude those who are suffering, personally, or through the illness of a relative. Churches need to put forward an image of a compassionate God who has been through history, and still is, drawing close to a broken world, revealing his glory even through pain.

Helping with the painful feelings brought about by caring

As chapter 2 has shown, many carers experience a range of conflicting and disturbing feelings. To see someone whose life is bound close to yours through ties of blood, marriage or friendship, suffering physical pain or handicap, can provoke intense grief. Countless tears are shed, outwardly and inwardly. Loss is a common feeling.

Added to this sense of grief and loss is often a great sense of anger and frustration. Anger is directed at fate, or, for the Christian, God. Frustration is a response too to over-demanding relatives. It is a reaction to the neglect of friends who could be sharing the responsibility for caring. Finally, it is reflection of the powerlessness felt by many carers, who see their lives slipping out of their control and becoming dominated, through the absence of effective support, by the caring situation.

To harbour such angry thoughts can, of course, lead to feelings of guilt and worthlessness. So can the feeling that one is not doing enough, that one is somehow falling short of the perfect, loving carer one aspires to be. Another feeling, worth remembering at this point, is the constant anxiety felt by many carers. For some the future is blank and it is also easy to fret over what would happen to your relative should you, by some mishap, no longer be able to care for them. There is anxiety over the illness, too, and the services being offered, anxiety over money, anxiety over the practical tasks demanding attention.

All these feelings, of grief, anger, guilt and anxiety, are heightened by the perpetual tiredness of many carers. Many of the people Jesus encountered in the course of his ministry were harrassed, tired and hurting. His response of compassion, patience and hope is to be mirrored by his Church. The comfort and relief he offered is mediated today through Christians.

Many churches have shown a desire to engage in the ministry of counselling in the 1980s and 1990s. Those who have become involved have recognised that helping those with complex emotional difficulties is no easy matter. Considerable training and supervision is needed if churches are to avoid harming people who are vulnerable. As a result Christians wishing to help carers on an emotional level need to be wise in the help they offer. It may be that local churches have a pre-existing professional counselling ministry. In this case, it may be advisable to refer needy carers to a trusted counsellor for guidance.

Where a church has little experience or skill in counselling, however, I would suggest that it avoid taking an active therapeutic role in assisting carers. The result, otherwise, might be to stir up and bring to the surface feelings which cannot be handled. The carers to whom I speak are, on the whole, not looking to fellow Christians for therapy, but for support. Consequently, churches such as those involved in CARELINK have concluded that a more passive, listening role is the most appropriate for them to assume.

A further role with which churches have felt comfortable is in facilitating self-help groups for carers. Recognising that many carers draw strength and encouragement from speaking to people who share their concerns, these churches have established their own carers support groups, which meet regularly, perhaps in a church member's lounge, to talk through their feelings and practical difficulties. Judy Wilson has written a useful book giving tips on setting up carers' support groups.(4)

A number of voluntary and statutory groups have decided

upon a telephone helpline as a means of meeting carers' emotional, among other, needs. Churches, too, particularly in the South West, have become involved in offering help over the phone to needy people.

Enabling relationships for carers

In chapter 4 we took a close look at some of the ways in which carers lose out socially.

Many strains occur in relationships as a result of caring. The balance of give and take in the relationship between a carer and their sick relative is upset. Often there is a role reversal, when a daughter or son takes up a 'parental' role towards their own mother or father. Tensions and irritation can be the result of spending many hours confined together at home. In addition, the carer can experience a sense of conflicting loyalties in other relationships, feeling they are giving insufficient time to close friends and relatives outside the caring relationship. Alternatively, there can be a sense of having been let down by relatives the carer feels are not pulling their weight.

Outside the family, contacts with the outside world are reduced. Often work has to be given up, and friendships with former colleagues are difficult to sustain. Old friends can feel too embarrassed to visit the carer for fear of saying the wrong thing. All too frequently the carer becomes isolated, their vital need to meet, mix with and talk to other people overlooked.

The problems in relationships experienced by carers require careful handling by churches. Helpers can be sucked so quickly into taking sides with the carer. In cases where both carer and cared-for person have connections with a church, it is especially important that those trying to help remain neutral and persist in seeing any disputes that arise from the perspective of both parties.

In situations where the carer's relationship with one or other of their relatives or friends has broken down, there may be an opportunity for a sensitive Christian to help reconcile the two, bringing them together again. A minister may find he is thrust into this role without necessarily seeking it. Consummate diplomacy and an attentiveness to the promptings of the Holy Spirit are required. A word of caution is needed at this point. It is crucial that Chrisitians recognise when they are out of their depth in handling conflicts, particularly in marriages, and are prepared to refer those in difficulty to specially trained agencies, such as Relate (formerly the Marriage Guidance Council). Really, there is little that can be done on a structured level to help carers in their relationships with kin. It is helpful, however, to be perpetually vigilant, looking out for instances in conversation when impartiality is demanded.

More can be done to alleviate the sense of isolation so prevalent amongst carers. Providing support groups helps not only emotionally, as we saw in the last section, but also in providing a social outlet for carers. Many carers have struck deep, long-lasting friendships through carers' support groups. Groups have experimented with holding numerous social functions. The mere anticipation of a regular meeting has been sufficient to keep lonely carers going.

It is important to remember that not all carers like to spend their 'time off' with others in the same position. Some prefer an activity totally removed from what they spend every other hour of the week doing. For those who would benefit from a support group, several considerations must be made. For a large proportion of carers, the existence of a support group is meaningless if no one is available to take care of their relative while they attend meetings. The absence of transport also presents an obstacle for many carers. A church initiating a support group might, therefore, need to provide sitters and cars as a pre-requisite. They would also have to think carefully about the venue they used. A cold room with uncomfortable seats and no facilities for making drinks hardly presents an attractive proposition. I think I would rather stay at home!

A support group does not represent the only alternative for meeting carers' social needs. The Congregational Church in Walkden (see later) has been successful in initiating a drop-in coffee morning for carers, where they can take a break from their shopping to meet other carers, people from the church and professionals. Many churches have been developed or rebuilt in recent years to provide comfortable, attractive halls and lounges, often with catering facilities. If these premises are left vacant during the week, the church is perhaps guilty of wasting its resources. How much better to open the doors to groups like carers who lack social settings in which to meet and talk informally with others. Financial implications are few, particularly if the coffee morning is run by volunteers and small charges are made for drinks and biscuits.

The opportunities for helping carers socially are endless. Churches have experimented successfully with 'befriending' schemes for different sections of the congregation. How many young students, away from home for the first time, have appreciated the warmth of Christian families near their college who have offered hospitality? Perhaps a similar scheme could be adapted for carers who wish to expand their circle of friends. They could be matched with single people, or families, who want to open their hearts and homes to offer friendship. Anyone involved in this type of initiative, however, must carefully appraise the time and energy they have to spare, to avoid raising the hopes of carers, only to dash those hopes by failing to sustain interest.

The value of a sitting service in meeting carers' needs for a break will be discussed in the next section. Suffice it to mention that an indirect benefit of such a relief scheme is that it allows carers to get out and meet up with friends.

A drop-in coffee morning for carers at Walkden Congregational Church, Worsley

Walkden Congregational Church, in the Salford area of Manchester, can testify to just how much can be achieved when local churches get together with agencies like Social Services departments to talk about the needs of local people.

The church has always felt that caring for people can prove to be a dramatic manifestation of God's kingdom of love. In all sorts of ways, they have demonstrated to local people that there is a God in heaven who cares about them. One or two years ago discussions with the local Social Services department revealed a need which it was felt the church could meet.

The Social Services department had initiated a support group for local carers. It met of an evening in council offices and seemed to be popular with carers. There was a problem, however. The offices provided a rather official, formal environment for what was intended to be a relaxed, social meeting. This was where the church came in.

It was felt that a church coffee room would be a more appropriate setting for the group. The Congregational Church was close to the shopping centre of the town and therefore easily accessible. Michael Durber, the minister of the church, was more than happy to suggest the group move over to the coffee room of the church. He recognised that caring can be an isolating experience. He could also see that there were many practical and emotional problems with which carers needed help. His inclination was to help other groups in responding to these needs.

Those concerned felt the timing of meetings had to be flexible to suit the needs of all those wishing to involve themselves. Tuesday morning between 10.00 am and 12.00 noon was selected as an ideal time and publicity made clear that carers were to feel at liberty simply to 'drop in' whenever and for whatever length of time was convenient.

Gradually, as the existence of the coffee morning became known, the numbers attending grew. Eventually, an average of 20 carers were popping in each week, some staying over an hour, others only a few minutes. It was good for them to be able to talk through with each other the experiences of the past week, to feel that others understood and cared. This mutual support proved to be a significant factor in reducing stress. The coffee morning additionally countered the loneliness and isolation many carers had been feeling.

Professionals continued to be involved, as did those working in local voluntary groups. They saw the coffee morning as an opportunity to pass on to carers vital information about the help available to them. It was also useful for professionals to be present in the respect that they were able to monitor the concerns of carers – a factor helpful in the development of policy.

Two issues remain a concern for Revd Durber. First of all, he realises that there are many carers – especially young carers – who have not been reached. He is attempting to find ways of contacting them. His second concern is that the church building which is used for meetings is in a state of disrepair and will need rebuilding before too long.

On the whole, though, he feels satisfied that the church is contributing to the efforts of other organisations in relieving the stress and isolation felt by carers in the area. He sees ways in which the church can co-operate with other groups in the future, perhaps caring for parents in especial need. For him, caring for the local community is fundamental to the church's work of spreading the Gospel. As he draws alongside carers on Tuesday mornings, he feels he is evidencing in some small way the love of a compassionate, attentive God.

Giving carers a break

Because family caring often takes place in one's home, it can be difficult to escape from it to take a rest or engage in relaxing pursuits. Fifty-seven per cent of the 1.5 million carers looking after someone in their own home, according to one survey, have had no break of at least two days since they started caring.(5) There are few opportunities for carers to take a break, and this situation is exacerbated by the fact that the carer is often unwilling to let go and allow someone else to take over for a few hours or a few days. It may also be difficult because the disabled relative will not accept willingly the care of another person, be they familiar or a stranger.

CARELINK is a scheme which aims to meet the carer's need for time off by providing a trusted friend for the disabled person. Sitting services, as schemes of this kind are called, cannot be initiated lightly. They require a high degree of commitment to visit regularly, punctually and faithfully. They often function best if volunteers are paid for their services. In most cases, a modicum of training for volunteers (in such things as the dynamics in the relationship between the disabled person and their carer, in first aid, in listening skills, in how to react in emergencies, and the like) is required. Finally, volunteers should receive careful support and supervision. Clearly the role of co-ordinator is very strategic in successfully matching volunteers with families and in giving continuing support to volunteers.(6)

Sitting services give carers a break of a few hours. In offering a slightly longer break, family placements have proved beneficial in contexts such as Social Services departments. They are often operated along the lines of a foster scheme. A family with skills in helping disabled people is carefully selected as a 'foster family' for the carer's disabled relative. They are often paid by the local authority involved.

Is there any way in which this type of idea could be mirrored in churches? In every church there are individuals skilled, either through their professional lives or experiences of caring, in looking after sick or disabled people. They could possibly get together in agreeing to offer caring families support. This would entail giving the disabled person a weekend or so's hospitality, thus allowing their family a rest and the chance to take a holiday.

This would have the benefit of bringing stimulation, friendship and variety into the life of the disabled person.

There are further ways for churches to give carers a change of scene and a rest. A group of families, including a caring family, could holiday together. That way some of the caring duties could perhaps be shared. The carer could also be relieved of practical tasks such as cooking meals and washing clothes. For some carers, the income from benefits on which they live does not stretch to allowing them to take holidays. In this case, it may be that their church could offer financial support.

I recently heard of a church which had recognised that one of its carers was struggling through lack of sleep. The carer was required to tend to the needs of their disabled relative during the night and their sleep was, therefore, interrupted. A group of people from the church took it upon themselves to spend a night each at the carer's home, looking after the disabled person through the hours of darkness, thus allowing the carer much-needed rest. This might be an idea other churches could copy quite easily.

Offering practical help

Many churches take very seriously their commitment to frail older members of their congregation. I am frequently impressed by the level of support such elderly folk receive from fellow Christians. Many are given lifts in church members' cars; some have help with their gardening and housework; others rely on Christian friends to help them with shopping. This practical help is, for some, the only factor allowing them to remain living in their own home.

In simple ways, these forms of assistance could be offered to carers too. A transport scheme where church members offer their vehicles for the use of those with no car, could be made available to them. Perhaps one church member could be appointed to co-ordinate the efforts of these volunteer drivers. They would, however, need to look carefully into the insurance position of these drivers.

Churches across the country are establishing 'care groups'. In essence, these are groups of church members willing to help people in their community with a range of practical tasks. In commending this idea, a church leader recently remarked wryly to me that volunteers need to carry round with them a pair of rubber gloves! You may have church members who are skilled in, and enjoy, gardening. Many carers struggle to maintain their gardens on top of the many other demands upon their time. Perhaps a task force of volunteers could offer help in the garden?

Some practical tasks around the house are overlooked by over-stretched carers too. Sensitivity is needed in offering help, but suggesting doing some washing, ironing, cleaning, mending, or cooking, could be something a team of volunteers could consider. For older carers, whose spouse becomes incapacitated, there are often tasks with which they are unfamiliar and now faced with completing. Perhaps their wife has always done the cooking, or it may be that their husband always paid the bills. Kind, sensitive help might be appropriate. Finally, a care group might be willing to undertake to do shopping for a stressed carer, or to collect a prescription.

Some care groups are organised on a neighbourhood basis, with members responsible for those living in their street. In this way a carer could be given peace of mind through being assured that a neighbour is on hand should they need assistance of one kind or another.

Another useful role churches can play is in ensuring that carers receive information about the services available to them. Some schemes, run by Social Services departments, the health authority, or voluntary groups, are under-used by carers. This might be because the carer is unaware that the help exists. In simple ways, churches could convey information about such services to carers. Church and parish magazines could carry advertisements. Churches could display details on their notice boards. They could even invite a representative of a scheme to speak briefly at a church meeting about the facility which they offer. One church is even the home to an information and advice service to carers in London, Waltham Forest Carers' Support Group. Based at the St Andrew's Christian Centre, Walthamstow, it is funded partly by the Church Urban Fund. The Support Group has produced an information pack and sends regular newsletters to carers in the borough.

The most widespread service offering practical help and regular breaks to carers is Crossroads Care Attendant Schemes.(7)

Though each is independent, with its unique structure, most towns and cities possess a scheme. They supply a care attendant for several hours each week who will go into the carer's home and take over while the carer has a break. They usually agree to perform whatever tasks in terms of caring, or practical work around the house, which the carer would have done. It is a highly valued service. In Dorset, a number of Christians have been involved in setting up similar Care Attendant Schemes, under the umbrella of an organisation called PRAMA. Though also spending time in the homes of disabled people living alone, these schemes, each run by a Christian nurse, help carers too. Setting up a care attendant scheme, be it independent, or under the auspices of Crossroads, is an ambitious project, but one which PRAMA have proved is possible.

In closing

In the context of discussing the possibilities for establishing church-based schemes for assisting carers, mention of the current political climate is needed.

The potential for churches to become involved in providing projects giving support to vulnerable people has perhaps never been greater this century than it is in the 1990s. This is an outcome of emphasis within social policy in recent years on Care in the Community. More specifically, it is a consequence of the National Health Service and Community Care Act of 1990. Under this Act, local authorities will become the agencies responsible for co-ordinating care, within local communities, for the frail elderly, those with mental illness and learning disabilities, and physically disabled children and adults. In assessing needs and co-ordinating this support, they are being asked to hand over, in large measure, their direct caring responsibilities to the so-called 'independent' sector.

In the years leading into the twenty-first century, therefore, we can expect to see local authority residential homes passing into the management of voluntary groups and private companies. We can anticipate that Social Services departments will, less and less, be going into people's homes to provide practical help. Already local authorities are turning to some churches, asking them to draw up contracts to provide a service to a vulnerable group. They are offering to pay churches to provide care to their own specifications to various groups.

In this climate, it is crucial that churches develop a firm idea of their 'calling'. Each church faced with the opportunity to become involved formally in providing care in the community will need to assess whether or not this activity falls within the mission to which they have been called. Outside help may be needed in reaching such a decision, in which case consulting with Christian organisations such as the Shaftesbury Society, with experience of Care in the Community, might be helpful.(8)

Whatever the level of support for carers to which your church becomes committed, it is my hope that responding to the very real practical and emotional needs they face will increasingly become a natural outworking of your corporate faith. Acting on the God-given impulse to protect those who hurt, I hope each of us as Christians will reflect the love of a Messiah whose call was, 'Come to me, all you who are weary and burdened, and I will give you rest' (Matthew 11:28).

References

1. Barbara Roberts, Report of a Project to Consider the Needs of Carers, Watford and District Association for Church Social Work (available from CARELINK, All Saints Hall, Gosforth Lane, South Oxhey, Hertfordshire WD1 6AX, 081 420 1568).
2. Jubilee Centre video, Carers: Out of Sight, Out of Mind, (for sale or hire from Jubilee Centre, 3 Hooper Street, Cambridge CB1 2NZ, 0223 311596), 1990.
3. Elisabeth Davies-Johns, It's More Than Installing a Ramp; Ministry Alongside Those With Disabilities, Methodist Publishing House, 1990.
4. Judy Wilson, Caring Together; Guidelines for Carers' Self-Help and Support Groups, King's Fund, 1988.
5. OPCS, General Household Survey 1985, HMSO, 1988.
6. Jill Pitkeathley, Working with Volunteers: Support, The Volunteer Centre UK, 1986.
Lesley Edmonds, Volunteers: A Resource for Your Church, The Volunteer Centre UK, 1988.
7. Crossroads, 10 Regent Place, Rugby, Warwickshire CV21 2PN, 0788 573653.
8. Community Involvement Pack, Shaftesbury Society (available from Shaftesbury Society, 18–20 Kingston Road, London SW19 1JZ, 081 542 5550), 1991.

Useful reading

Caring, and how to help carers

Mary Craig, *Blessings* (autobiographical), Hodder and Stoughton, 1979.

Jubilee Centre video, *Carers; Out of Sight, Out of Mind*, (available for sale or hire from: Jubilee Centre, 3 Hooper Street, Cambridge CB1 2NZ, 0223 311596), 1990.

Anna Briggs and Judith Oliver, *Caring: Experiences of Looking After Disabled Relatives*, Routledge and Kegan Paul, 1985.

Judy Wilson, *Caring Together; Guidelines for Carers' Self-Help and Support Groups*, King's Fund, 1988.

Margaret Forster, *Have the Men Had Enough?* (a novel), Chatto and Windus, 1989.

Jill Pitkeathley, *It's My Duty, Isn't It? The Plight of Carers in Our Society*, Souvenir Press, 1989.

Maggie Jee, *Living with M.S.; A Guide for Carers, Families and Friends*, King's Fund, 1989.

Caroline Philps, *'Mummy, Why Have I Got Down's Syndrome?'* (autobiographical), Lion Publishing, 1991.

Robert Davis, *My Journey Into Alzheimer's Disease; Helpful Insights for Family and Friends* (autobiographical), Tyndale House Publishers (USA), 1989.

Ann Richardson, Judith Unell and Beverly Aston, *A New Deal for Carers*, King's Fund, 1989.

Brenda Baalham, *One in a Million* (autobiographical), Lutterworth Press, 1991.

Mary Moate and Dr David Enoch, *Schizophrenia; Voices in the Dark* (partly autobiographical), Kingsway, 1990.

Julia Burton-Jones, *Serving Carers; A Handbook for You and Your Church*, Jubilee Centre Publications (address as above), 1990.

Hazel Morgan, *Through Peter's Eyes* (autobiographical), Arthur James, 1990.

Rosie Bell and Sue Gibbons, *Working With Carers; Information and Training for Work With Informal Carers*, Health Education Authority, 1989.

Advice for carers

Sharon Fish, *Alzheimer's: Caring for Your Loved One, Caring for Yourself*, Lion Publishing, 1991.

Mary Craig, *Blessings* (autobiographical), Hodder and Stoughton, 1979.

Christine Orton, *Care for the Carer; Make Life Easier, Happier and More Fulfilling for You and the Elderly Person You Look After*, Thorsons Publishing, 1989.

Nancy Kohner, *Caring at Home; A Handbook for People Looking After Someone at Home – Someone Young or Old, Handicapped or Disabled, Ill or Frail*, King's Fund, 1988.

David Yelding, *Caring for Someone With AIDS; A Clear Practical Guide for People Coping With AIDS, Including Where to Go for Information and Support*, Hodder and Stoughton, 1990.

Jane Brotchie, *Help at Hand; The Home Carer's Survival Guide*, Bedford Square Press, 1990.

Betty Kershaw, Stephen G Wright and Pauline Hammonds, *Helping to Care; A Handbook for Carers at Home and in Hospital*, Bailliere Tindall, 1989.

Royal Association for Disability and Rehabilitation, *Holidays in the British Isles; A Guide for Disabled People*, 1991.

Royal Association for Disability and Rehabilitation, *Holidays and Travel Abroad; A Guide for Disabled People*, 1991.

Maggie Jee, *Living With M.S.; A Guide for Carers, Families and Friends*, King's Fund, 1989.

Caroline Philps, *'Mummy, Why Have I Got Down's Syndrome?'* (autobiographical), Lion Publishing, 1991.

Sally Burningham, *Not on Your Own; the MIND Guide to Mental Health*, Penguin, 1989.

Diana Kimpton, *A Special Child in the Family; Living With Your Sick or Disabled Child*, Sheldon Press/SPCK, 1990.

Fuller Torrey, *Surviving Schizophrenia; a Family Manual*, Harper and Row, 1985.

Taking a Break; A Guide for People Caring at Home, Health Education Authority (available from the King's Fund) 1987.

Hazel Morgan, *Through Peter's Eyes* (autobiographical), Arthur James, 1990.

On disability and old age

Pat Saunders, *The A-Z of Disability; Directory of Information, Services, Organisations, Equipment and Manufacturers*, Crowood Press, 1989.

A Report of the Church of England Board for Social Responsibility, *Ageing*, Church House Publishing, 1990.

Christian Awareness Pack; Mental Handicap, Causeway (PO Box 351, Reading, Berkshire, RG1 7AL, 0734 508781), 1990.

Julia Burton-Jones, *From Generation to Generation; Towards a Christian Understanding of the Role and Care of Older People*, Jubilee Centre Publications (address above), 1990.

Royal Association for Disability and Rehabilitation, *Holidays in the British Isles; A Guide for Disabled People*, 1991.

Royal Association for Disability and Rehabilitation, *Holidays and Travel Abroad; A Guide for Disabled People*, 1991.

Elisabeth Davies-Johns, *It's More Than Installing a Ramp; Ministry Alongside Those With Disabilities*, Methodist Publishing House, 1990.

Ann Webber, *Life Later On; Older People and the Church*, Triangle/SPCK, 1990.

Do-it-Yourself Pack, *The Local Church and People With Mental Handicaps*, Scripture Union Training Unit and Cause for Concern (available from SU Training Unit, 26–30 Heathcoat Street, Nottingham NG1 3AA, 0602 418144), 1990.

Martyn Eden, David Potter and Terry Thompson, *No Handicaps, Please; We're Christians*, Causeway (address above), 1990.

Sally Burningham, *Not on Your Own; the MIND Guide to Mental Health*, Penguin, 1989.

Mary Moate and Dr David Enoch, *Schizophrenia; voices in the Dark* (partly autobiographical), Kingsway, 1990.

Patrick Slack and Frank Mulville, *Sweet Adeline; A Journey Through Care*, MacMillan, 1988.

David and Madeleine Potter, *We're All Special to God; A Resource for Groups of People With Mental Handicaps*, Scripture Union, 1990.

Community involvement

Do-it-Yourself Pack, *Christian Caring; A Do-it-Yourself Training Course in Helping Skills*, Scripture Union Training Unit (address above), 1989.

Community Involvement Pack, Shaftesbury Society (18–20 Kingston Road, London SW19 1JZ, 081 542 5550), 1991.

Sandy Adirondack and Richard Macfarlane, *Getting Ready for Contracts; A Guide for Voluntary Organisations*, Directory of Social Change, 1990.

Lesley Edmonds, *Volunteers; A Resource for Your Church*, Volunteer Centre UK, 1988.

Useful organisations

Groups working with carers

Carers National Association (national charity for carers)
29 Chilworth Mews
London W2 3RG
071 724 7776

King's Fund Carers Unit (providing publications and helping develop local
support for carers)
126 Albert Street
London NW1 7NF
071 267 6111

Contact a Family (for parents of disabled children)
16 Strutton Ground
Victoria
London SW1P 2HP
071 222 2695

Crossroads Care (national association of care attendant schemes)
10 Regent Place
Rugby
Warwickshire CV21 2PN
0788 573653

Alzheimer's Disease Society
158/160 Balham High Road
London SW12 9BN
081 675 6557

Some of the larger groups working with disabled people

Age Concern England
Astral House
1268 London Road
London SW16 4ER
081 679 8000

Age Concern Scotland
33 Castle Street
Edinburgh EH2 3DN
031 225 5000

Age Concern Wales
1 Cathedral Road
Cardiff CF1 9SD
0222 371821

Cancerlink
17 Britannia Street
London WC1X 9JN
071 833 2451

Counsel and Care for the Elderly
Twyman House
16 Bonny Street
London NW1 9PG
071 485 1550

Disability Alliance
25 Denmark Street
London WC2H 8NJ
071 240 0806

Disablement Information and Advice Line (DIAL)
117 High Street
Clay Cross
Chesterfield
Derbyshire S45 9DZ
0246 250055

Disabled Living Foundation
380–384 Harrow Road
London W9 2HU
071 289 6111

Mencap (Royal Society for Mentally Handicapped Children and Adults)
125 Golden Lane
London EC1Y 0RT
071 253 9437

MIND (National Association for Mental Health)
22 Harley Street
London W1N 2ED
071 637 0741

Spastics Society
12 Park Crescent
London W1N 4EQ
071 636 5020

Groups supporting voluntary organisations

National Association of Councils for Voluntary Service
Third Floor, Arundel Court
177 Arundel Street
Sheffield S1 2NU
0742 786636

National Association for Volunteer Bureaux
St Peter's College
College Road
Saltley
Birmingham B8 3TE
021 327 0265

Community Development Foundation
60 Highbury Grove
London N5 2AG
071 226 5375

Directory of Social Change
Radius Works
Back Lane
London NW3 1HL
071 435 8171

National Council of Voluntary Organisations
26 Bedford Square
London WC1B 3HU
071 636 4066

The National Self-Help Support Centre
26 Bedford Square
London WC1B 3HU
071 636 4066

The Volunteer Centre UK
29 Lower King's Road
Berkhamsted
Hertfordshire HP4 2AB
0442 873311

Christian groups working with disabled people and their carers

The Christian Council on Ageing
Membership Secretary
20 West Way
Rickmansworth
Hertfordshire WD3 2EN
0923 774998

A Cause for Concern: Expressing Christian Concern for People With Mental
Handicaps
PO Box 351
Reading
Berkshire RG1 7AL
0734 508781

Association for the Pastoral Care of the Mentally Ill: An Association Which
Supports the Mentally Ill and Their Relatives
351 City Road
London EC1N 4BJ
071 278 3438

Church Action on Disability
Revd John Pierce (Secretary)
Charisma Cottage
Drewsteignton
Exeter EX6 6QR
0647 21259

The Shaftesbury Society (providing residential and community services for
disabled people)
18–20 Kingston Road
London SW19 1JZ
081 542 5550

Disabled Christians' Fellowship
50 Clare Road
Kingswood
Bristol
Avon BS15 1PJ
0232 616141

Scripture Union Training Unit (resourcing the local church)
26–30 Heathcoat Street
Nottingham NG1 3AA
0602 418144

Action for Family Carers
c/o Scripture Union Training Unit (address above)

Christian Project Developments Ltd
154 Loughborough Road
West Bridgford
Nottingham NG2 7JE
0602 255485